SOA Governance

The key to successful SOA adoption in
your organization

Todd Biske

PUBLISHING

BIRMINGHAM - MUMBAI

SOA Governance

The key to successful SOA adoption in your organization

First published: October 2008

Production Reference: 1061008

Published by Packt Publishing Ltd.
32 Lincoln Road
Olton
Birmingham, B27 6PA, UK.

ISBN 978-1-847195-86-9

www.packtpub.com

Cover Image by Nilesh Mohite (nilpreet2000@yahoo.co.in)

Credits

Author

Todd Biske

Reviewers

Swaminathan Chandrasekaran

William Laurent

Acquisition Editors

Sarah Cullington

Adil Ahmed

Technical Editor

Dhiraj Chandiramani

Editorial Team Leader

Akshara Aware

Project Manager

Abhijeet Deobhakta

Project Coordinator

Leena Purkait

Indexer

Monica Ajmera

Proofreader

Laura Booth

Production Coordinator

Shantanu Zagade

Cover Work

Shantanu Zagade

About the Author

Todd Biske is a Senior Enterprise Architect with Monsanto in St. Louis, Missouri. He has over 15 years of experience in Information Technology, both as a corporate practitioner and as a consultant, working with companies involved with Agriculture, Atmospheric Sciences, Financial Services, Insurance, and Travel and Leisure. His interests include Service-Oriented Architecture, Systems Management Technologies, Usability, and Human-Computer Interaction. He has a M.S. degree in Computer Science from the University of Illinois at Urbana-Champaign, is a member of the SOA Consortium, is a frequent conference presenter, and writes a popular blog on strategic IT topics at http://www.biske.com/blog/.

When Todd isn't working or blogging, he spends the vast majority of his time enjoying life with his wife Andrea, and their three children, Elena, Spencer, and Maria. This typically involves one or more of the following (sometimes simultaneously): assisting in the construction of Lego spaceships and vehicles, playing various Wii games, coaching baseball teams, watching soccer games, cheering for the St. Louis Cardinals, attending Broadway musicals when they come through town, and maybe, if there's any time left (there usually isn't) reading some good fiction.

There are many people I'd like to thank. First, I thank my colleagues at Monsanto for their support of this effort. Second, a big thank you to Brenda Michelson and the SOA Consortium for advice and conversation. Third, I thank my past colleagues and friends at previous jobs, for without those experiences this book would not have been possible. Fourth, I'd like to thank the staff at Packt Publishing, including Adil Ahmed, Patricia Weir, Leena Purkait, and Sarah Cullington for their assistance in this effort. Finally, and most importantly, I thank my wife and family for encouraging me to take this challenge on, and for their sacrifice of family time so that this book could become a reality.

About the Reviewers

Swami Chandrasekaran a Senior SOA Solutions Architect with IBM, has more than 12 years of progressive experience in the areas focused on strategy, architecture, implementation, and delivery of large scale strategic IT solutions. His credits include technical and strategic interface with various senior executive and institutions, including Fortune 100/500 companies, U.S. and international clients.

In his current role at IBM, as a visionary and senior member of the client services organization, he leads pre-sales, architecture and design of service-oriented applications for their key clients and partners. He is also the Co-Lead Architect and SME for the WebSphere Business Services Fabric Telecom Content Pack product.

His current areas of passion include Service Oriented and Composite Applications, Semantic Web, Next Generation Service Delivery Platforms, and Enterprise Architecture Visualization. He lives with his family in Dallas, TX and during his free time he blogs at http://blog.nirvacana.com. He has authored several articles featured in "BearingPoint Institute for Thought Leadership" and also hold several patent disclosures. He previously worked for BearingPoint and also for Ericsson Wireless Research. Swami hold's a Bachelor's and Master's degree in Electrical Engineering.

William Laurent is one of the world's leading experts in information strategy, and Business Intelligence and Governance. For more than 15 years he has advised numerous companies and governments on technology strategy, methodologies, and best practices. He is a regularly featured writer and columnist for DM Review where he writes about IT and corporate governance. In addition, he serves as Contributing Editor for Dashboard Insight. William has taught at Baruch College and Columbia University. He runs an independent consulting company that bears his name, and lectures frequently on various technology and business topics worldwide.
Mr. Laurent is the former President of National Information Management and currently resides in New York City metro area and Tokyo Japan. He would enjoy your comments at wlaurent@williamlaurent.com.

Much thanks goes out to my family for their constant encouragement and optimism; especially to Rion for her love; to my mentors in Japan and the USA; and to Glen Michael.

Table of Contents

Preface

In order to provide appropriate context for the concepts and techniques that can help you implement appropriate SOA Governance, this book will tell a story of a fictional company, Advasco. You will follow key members of the company, including:

- Andrea, the CIO of Advasco
- Spencer, an Enterprise Architect
- Elena, the Chief Architect
- Maria, the Service Manager

In each chapter, you will hear a portion of their journey on the path to SOA adoption. Following the narrative of their experiences will be an explanation of the situations that arose for Advasco, along with the role that SOA Governance played in the scenario, either through the lack of it, or through the successful application of people, policies, and process.

What This Book Covers

Chapter 1 will introduce you to the concept of governance, using the familiar concept of municipal government, introduce its core components of people, policies, and processes, and then illustrate why these are important to the adoption of SOA within an enterprise.

Chapter 2 will introduce you to the beginning of Advasco's SOA journey, and their initial experiences building and consuming services.

In *Chapter 3*, you will find out what ensues when Advasco tries to expand on its initial successes after some recognition and encouragement from Andrea, the CIO.

Chapter 4 will take you through the experiences of Advasco when one of their production services needs to be upgraded to a new version and support the needs of a new consumer.

Chapter 5 brings Advasco to the inevitable let down after its initial success and addresses the steps that the company takes to keep the SOA effort progressing forward.

Chapter 6 explores the world of run-time SOA governance by discussing the activities of Advasco after a bug in a service is exposed in the production environment.

In *Chapter 7*, the changes that have occurred in Advasco over the course of their SOA journey are summarized.

Finally, *Chapter 8* provides a detailed overview of both the techniques explored in the Advasco story, as well as other options available to you and your organization.

The *Appendix* shows a list of characters that appear in the Advasco story, their role, and the chapters in which they appear.

Conventions

In this book, you will find a number of styles of text that distinguish between different kinds of information. Here are some examples of these styles, and an explanation of their meaning.

A block of code will be set as follows:

```
<wsu:Timestamp xmlns:wsu="http://docs.oasis-open.org/wss/2004/01/
               oasis-200401-wss-wssecurity-utility-1.0.xsd"
               wsu:Id="Timestamp-aaddaaf5-1207-44d7-a5ab-64b6bf5f678e">
<wsu:Created>2008-05-27T21:23:25Z</wsu:Created>
</wsu:Timestamp>
```

New terms and **important words** are introduced in a bold-type font.

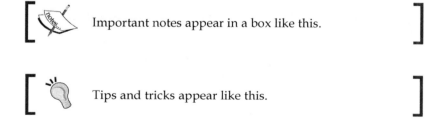

Important notes appear in a box like this.

Tips and tricks appear like this.

Reader Feedback

Feedback from our readers is always welcome. Let us know what you think about this book, what you liked or may have disliked. Reader feedback is important for us to develop titles that you really get the most out of.

To send us general feedback, simply drop an email to feedback@packtpub.com, making sure to mention the book title in the subject of your message.

If there is a book that you need and would like to see us publish, please send us a note in the **SUGGEST A TITLE** form on www.packtpub.com or email suggest@packtpub.com.

If there is a topic that you have expertise in and you are interested in either writing or contributing to a book, see our author guide on www.packtpub.com/authors.

Customer Support

Now that you are the proud owner of a Packt book, we have a number of things to help you to get the most from your purchase.

Errata

Although we have taken every care to ensure the accuracy of our contents, mistakes do happen. If you find a mistake in one of our books—maybe a mistake in text or code—we would be grateful if you would report this to us. By doing this you can save other readers from frustration, and help to improve subsequent versions of this book. If you find any errata, report them by visiting http://www.packtpub.com/support, selecting your book, clicking on the **let us know** link, and entering the details of your errata. Once your errata are verified, your submission will be accepted and the errata added to the list of existing errata. The existing errata can be viewed by selecting your title from http://www.packtpub.com/support.

Piracy

Piracy of copyright material on the Internet is an ongoing problem across all media. At Packt, we take the protection of our copyright and licenses very seriously. If you come across any illegal copies of our works in any form on the Internet, please provide the location address or website name immediately so we can pursue a remedy.

Please contact us at copyright@packtpub.com with a link to the suspected pirated material.

We appreciate your help in protecting our authors, and our ability to bring you valuable content.

Questions

You can contact us at questions@packtpub.com if you are having a problem with some aspect of the book, and we will do our best to address it.

1
The Essence of SOA Governance

What is governance? Why is it so critical to the success of an SOA adoption effort. This chapter will introduce you to the concept of governance, using the familiar concept of municipal government, introduce its core components of people, policies, and processes, and then illustrate why these are important to the adoption of SOA within an enterprise.

What is Governance?

When you hear the word "governance", what comes to mind? For most people in information technology, it is not a positive image. If you are a typical corporate developer, you are probably envisioning forms to fill out, presentations to prepare, meetings in front of a review board, and more than likely, annoyance in having to take time away from writing code for people that, in your opinion, really don't understand what you're trying to do in the first place. Often, a developer may see the review as nothing more than an opportunity for the reviewers to flaunt their authority. They simply take their lumps in the review, and then everybody goes back to doing what they were doing with no real change in behavior, other than some additional animosity in the organization.

If you are an enterprise architect, you may be on the other side of this equation. You are the one listening to presentations from project teams, trying to provide guidance to ensure that the efforts go beyond the needs of the individual project, but only encountering developers who are more interested in finding opportunities to try the newest technologies than what is needed to meet the needs of the enterprise. Even if the developers are able to be convinced, the required changes then get shot down by a project manager or sponsor who won't accept the resulting change in schedule.

If you are a manager, especially a senior manager, you may have a completely different take on governance. Rather than being about the efforts going on inside a project, it's about getting projects approved. Many organizations even have a committee called the **IT Governance Committee**, whose job is to review project proposals and determine which efforts will be funded. While there normally isn't as much pain associated with this effort, there's still potential for animosity when managers don't understand the prioritization process used by the committee.

So why do we do it? The fact is that governance is a required and critical part of any organization. It is the combination of people, policies, and processes that are put in place to ensure the organization achieves one or more desired behaviors. When used properly, it can be the difference between success and failure.

The adoption of **service-oriented architecture**, or **SOA**, has been touted as an approach that can change the way IT operates, increasing the agility of the organization and achieving a greater degree of alignment between IT and the rest of the business. An effort of this nature represents a fundamental change in the way an organization leverages information technology. It is up to governance to guide the organization through this change.

To better understand governance, let's first look at it from a different context, one that we all deal with on a daily basis, which is municipal government.

Desired Behavior

The city you live in is a living organization, trying to meet the needs of its constituents and businesses alike. Nearly all cities have a desired behavior of being a safe place where people want to raise their children and businesses want to operate. Cities will likely vary, however, in their approach to growth. At one end, an established city may be landlocked and may have to focus on remaining attractive to both young and old residents, keeping the population base stable. At the other end, areas near urban centers with plenty of open space may be experiencing rapid growth as young professionals seek larger lots with plenty of space for kids to play. In the middle, rural communities may be looking for slow, controlled growth to preserve their rural heritage yet remain attractive to young families.

People

Regardless of where you live, you are likely to be subjected to many forms of government. Your city or village may have a mayor and a city council. The churches may have a pastor and an associated council of leaders. Your city or village may be part of a regional government, such as a state or province with a governor or other form of provincial leadership. That regional government is likely to be subjected to the oversight of the country's government, which can include a president or prime minister, along with parliament, congress, or some other body of representatives. In addition to these roles, one cannot forget the police force. All of these examples have one thing in common: people who are recognized as authority figures, typically in either a position of establishing, or enforcing, policy.

It should be known, however, that authority does not necessarily imply a dictatorship. In many governments, it is the people that grant the authority figures their powers through the election process, and the people typically have the power to remove those figures from authority. While the typical corporation is not a democracy, there are many lessons to be learned from a democratic style of government. One must not forget that the motto of many police organizations is *to serve and protect*, while legislators are *representatives of the people*. The correct message is that governance is a responsibility of everyone, whether formally assigned or not. The degree to which the governed participate in the governance process can have a huge impact on the success or failure of the governance effort.

Policies

Simply having people is not enough. While the people may all agree on where they want to go, it is the policies associated with the day-to-day activities of the community that make it happen. The community must look at its desired behavior and determine the right set of policies that will achieve that behavior. For example, does the community want to be a bedroom community, or does it want to be a retail hub for the region? Does it want to focus on attracting medium to large organizations with many employees, or will it focus on smaller businesses? Will the community stay small, or will it be on a path of continued growth, adding property, businesses, and residents over time? Will the community allow a variety of residents and businesses, ranging from low income housing to million dollar mansions and from the local hardware store to a major international company? What kind of education will the community provide for its residents?

In order to ensure that the community realizes the desired behavior, its actions must be guided through policy. These policies will cover a range of things that are required for the community to stay healthy and grow. It involves many different aspects, including the speed limits on city streets, tax rates for residents and businesses, and zoning regulations that guide the types of businesses allowed. There are also polices that influence the activities that take place within the city, such as specifying that a specific percentage of revenue must go towards education versus other needs. It is likely that an IT Governance committee has similar policies that are used in determining which projects get funded.

Process

As the community grows and the policies grow more and more numerous, it will become clear that having people and policies alone are still inadequate for effective governance. While many people will adhere to policies, not everyone will. For some, it may be due to a deliberate action, for others, it may simply be due to lack of awareness. In order to combat this, processes must be put in place to ensure that the community is aware of the policies that have been created by the leaders, as well as processes that ensure that the community is following those policies.

Take, for example, speed limits. In its earliest phases a community may not have had any speed limits on its roads. Over time, as the community grows, a continued increase in the number of automobile accidents may cause the leaders to establish a speed limit on city roads: a policy. However, simply passing this law during a city council meeting is unlikely to change behavior. The first thing the leaders must do is educate the community on the new policy, and they do so by placing speed limit signs on the roads in question. In addition, a driver's education course is created and all new drivers, or drivers that are renewing their licenses, are required to complete it successfully before receiving their new or renewed license. These processes will certainly increase the adherence to the policy, but just as many drivers on the road today ignore speed limit signs and so it may not achieve the levels desired by the leader. To achieve the desired behavior, the city council decides that a police force is necessary to enforce the policies. Through the use of radar guns the police are able to detect when automobiles are out of compliance with the stated policies, and can institute appropriate punishment in the form of warnings, fines, or other loss of privileges.

Processes are frequently the difference between good governance and poor governance. All too often, the negative view of governance is a result of an over-emphasis on policy enforcement. This can frequently result in a command-and-control culture, which can create animosity in an organization. Perhaps, even more important than enforcement processes are communication and education processes. By educating the residents and businesses on the policies first, it is far easier to achieve compliance. Likewise, the authorities must have an open ear, and listen to where policies are actually counter-productive to the goals of the community. Finally, just as the people and businesses are held accountable for adherence to the policies, the authorities must be held accountable for their actions, with the people having the ability to remove leaders that are not acting in the best interest of the constituents or if the desired behaviors are not being achieved.

It is important to realize that no two governments are alike. In communities where the residents have a high degree of trust in the leaders, and agreement on the direction and policies, the community may not need as many enforcement processes as the residents naturally adhere to the policies as it is in their best interest. In communities where the residents do not trust the leaders of the organization, due to corruption or other factors, policies may not be followed, and as a result, the community may have to invest far more heavily in education and more likely, enforcement through the police force.

These aspects are the essence of governance: desired behavior, people, policies, and process. The desired behavior is achieved through a successful combination of people, policies, and processes. People are the leaders that are responsible for establishing the desired behavior of the organization, policies are the rules that express the desired behavior, and process ensures that the policies are followed. Just as no two governments will operate in exactly the same manner, with the same structure, the same holds true for information technology organizations. They will each have their own leadership structure, desired behavior, policies, and processes. If the desired behavior is being achieved, the governance is successful.

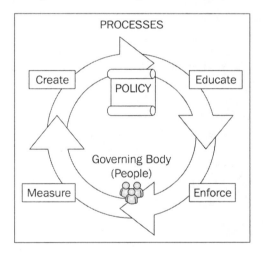

What is IT Governance?

While it easy to put governance into the context of municipal or regional governments, it is not limited to this domain. The *Sarbanes-Oxley Act* increased awareness of the term **corporate governance**. A key aspect of Sarbanes-Oxley was to ensure that the corporate boards (the people responsible for governance) of publicly-traded companies in the United States take individual responsibility for the accuracy and completeness of financial reports. In addition, there were new standards established for compliance audits of these companies. In order to be compliant, companies had to introduce new policies associated with a variety of corporate activities. On top of that, it was certainly in the company's best interest to perform their own audits and ensure compliance with these policies through internal processes prior to the official audits by an independent auditor. While Sarbanes-Oxley may not touch on all aspects of corporate governance, it certainly serves to demonstrate how people, policies, and processes are an inherent part.

In the case of Sarbanes-Oxley, the primary concern is governing the financial accounting practices, with the desired behavior being articulated as part of it. Another part of corporate governance, however, is the desired behavior of the use of information technology, which is known as IT Governance. Remaining consistent with the earlier definition of governance, IT Governance is defined as the people, policies, and processes that an organization leverages to ensure the appropriate behaviors and outcomes in respect to the organization's utilization of information technology. In many organizations, the face of IT Governance is the review board (people) that make decisions on which efforts receive funding, and which do not. However, IT governance does not end there. Many organizations also have **Portfolio Management Organizations**, or **PMOs**, that ensure that the efforts, once funded, are properly prioritized, staffed, and executed in a consistent and appropriate manner. The PMOs must establish policies that define what **consistent and appropriate** means, and then ensure that the projects are compliant with those policies.

What is SOA?

Before we delve into governance within the context of SOA, we first need to define what SOA is. The first step in this is to define what we mean by service. One of the many definitions provided by the Merriam-Webster dictionary (http://www.merriam-webster.com/) for service is *a facility supplying some public demand*. The key parts of this definition are **facility** which means that some capability or function is performed, **supplying** which means that the function is provided to consumers, and **public demand** which means it's something that one or more consumers actually want. A SOA, therefore, is quite simply, an architecture that utilizes the core concepts of service providers and service consumers to define a system.

Building on our example of a municipality, the community may initially have started as a collection of homes, each with their own well for water, garden for food, and so on. Over time, however, the residents realized the need for some common services. It may have begun with residents each contributing property for a common road that connects their houses. In other areas, it was likely focused on the economies of scale, such as a public school system, a shared source of water, sanitation services, and as technology evolved, communications and media services. As these services evolved, the impact on individual residents varied widely. Some residents had designed their homes in such a way that a transition from their private well to a public water source was an inexpensive effort. Other residents, however, had far greater expenses in adapting their internal plumbing to the fixtures required by the public source. The municipality can be viewed as a collection of these services, with the municipality acting as the provider of the services and its residents as the consumer of the services.

While this definition may seem simple, it captures the essence of what SOA is all about: breaking down a system into a collection of consumers and providers. The key to a successful SOA, however, is ensuring that the right services are provided and that the relationships between consumers and providers are formally established and managed. A city that has a complicated maze of pothole-laden roads, unreliable electricity, poor schools, high taxes, along with a city council that was appointed for life is not going to be a pleasant place to live. Are they providing services? Yes. Are they providing them well? No. Is the relationship between the constituents and city healthy, given that the council members are assured a paycheck for life, regardless of whether any improvements are made? Probably not.

Services in IT

If we compare this to the typical corporate IT department, individual applications are similar to the homesteads provided in a new community. Many of these applications are currently implementing capabilities in their own, private manner, even though there are many applications within the enterprise that implement the same capability. Some of these capabilities will be pure infrastructure, such as security and logging, but others will be business capabilities such as customer management and order processing.

Just as some of our homeowners had a higher cost associated with utilizing the public services, the same thing holds true in the world of corporate information technology. Many applications are hampered by an inflexible design such that the cost of change is now prohibitive. This shouldn't be considered a result of poor decisions taken years ago, but rather the normal course of growth. It is unlikely that all homeowners could have anticipated the changes that would happen over the years, and equally unlikely, if not more, that application designers could anticipate the technology advances that have occurred over the last twenty years.

One key difference between the typical corporate enterprise and typical community, however, is that all things in the enterprise exist for the good of the enterprise, and not as independent entities. When an individual homeowner chose to build in an inflexible manner, the only one impacted by this inflexibility was the homeowner. The community, as a whole, is likely not impacted by this. For the corporate enterprise, however, an inflexible application is another story. As long as that application is still necessary for the enterprise, the cost associated with that inflexibility will grow larger and larger. Just as a community can bulldoze a dilapidated property, an enterprise can choose to scrap an application and rewrite, but that comes at a large expense.

In order to prevent the continued cycle of inflexibility, an enterprise must move away from today's state where the information technology assets are largely viewed as a collection of individual applications and their data to a state where the assets are viewed as a collection of capabilities provided as services. This is a very important distinction, because many enterprises have simply taken existing applications, rewritten sections of them as services, and think that they're adopting SOA. When it comes down to it, however, they still have the same applications, and those applications still have the same integration challenges. For example, the typical enterprise has a collection of applications as shown in the following figure:

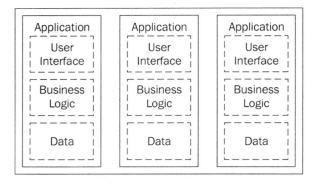

When the need arose for these applications to communicate, the generally accepted approach was to create an adapter that acts as the glue that connects the two applications. For each new pair of applications that need to be integrated, a new adapter would be created, adding more and more complexity over time.

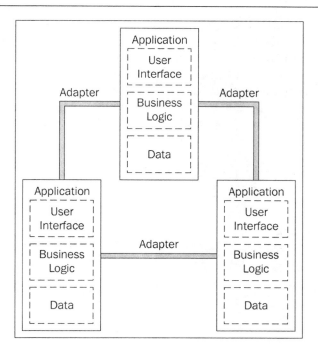

To get out of this endless cycle of adding more and more adapters in the middle, which adds complexity, the enterprise needs to move away from application oriented architecture. Application oriented architecture is where the core unit used to describe the enterprise is an application. It therefore follows that SOA, simply stated, is an architecture whose core unit of composition is a service. If we take the diagrams above and eliminate the boundaries of the application, we get a picture that looks like the following:

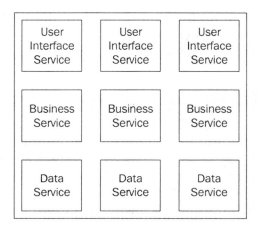

When these boundaries are eliminated, the enterprise can now be viewed as a collection of service consumers and service providers that are expected to operate as a community. This is instead of being viewed as a collection of individual applications that have no clear indication of where capabilities are shared, and inconsistent internal structures that do not support future change or integration needs. User interface components and all business logic services are built in a consistent, composable manner, and all data resources are exposed in a consistent, composable manner as shown in the following figure:

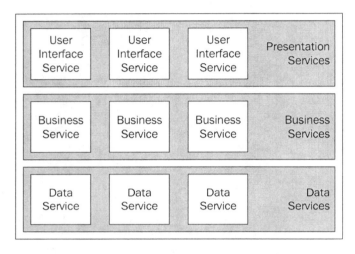

This approach doesn't prevent individual services from being highly customized for a particular need. What it does do, however, is to ensure that we still build for agility. If the end result is that a particular business service only has one consumer, that's still okay.

Adopting SOA and moving away from application oriented architecture will allow information technology to lead the enterprise to progress into the future, rather than being perceived as the anchor holding the enterprise back.

What is SOA Governance?

Given the understanding we now have of governance in general, and of service oriented architecture and the desired behaviors it intends to achieve, what is SOA governance and why is it important? SOA governance is the combination of people, policies, and processes within your organization that will ensure that the desired behaviors of your strategic SOA initiative are achieved.

It includes the traditional areas associated with IT Governance, which is the selection and funding of IT projects. These projects define the initial scope for technology utilization and can either help or hinder the SOA effort, based upon the scope chosen.

The SOA effort only gets executed through projects, and if the execution is poor, the SOA effort will be poor. Therefore, the project governance activities of an organization must be adjusted to include policies associated with achieving the desired behaviors associated with SOA adoption.

However, it doesn't stop there; the behavior of the IT solutions and the teams that support them may also require changes. The redefinition of boundaries associated with technology solutions can result in new operational activities and a greater need to respond quickly to changes without having a ripple effect through the systems. Run-time governance must be leveraged to ensure the systems and the organizations supporting them operate as efficiently as possible.

People

The people involved with SOA governance will mainly include the same people involved with your current IT and Project governance efforts. New artifacts may be required to help establish appropriate policies for SOA success. If the existing governance efforts are poor or unsuccessful, it may be necessary to bring in new people or a new approach to your governance efforts. Individuals involved will include senior leadership from both within and outside of IT, enterprise architects, technology architects, development managers, business architects/senior business analysts, and more. The SOA effort cannot be viewed as just an IT operation. While the IT department may oversee a significant portion of the SOA efforts, if those efforts are not in alignment with the desired behavior of the organization as a whole, conflict will arise. This would also be the case if a city was out of alignment with the state or province, or if the state or province was out of alignment with the federal government.

The constituents of the organization are both the IT staff involved in the construction of services and their consumers, the business users that utilize the IT solutions, and in many cases, an organization's partners that may interact via services.

Policies

The policies that the people involved with the SOA governance effort create must guide the organization towards the desired behavior of the SOA effort. If the effort is intended to reduce the costs associated with the typical IT development effort, what are the policies that will result in that outcome? If the effort is intended to reduce the time required to make system changes in response to regulatory changes that occur on a regular basis, what are the policies that will result in the outcome? What are the policies that will ensure that the SOA adoption effort won't have a negative effect on the organization by the resulting increase in moving parts putting new strains on inefficient operational processes? If the organization simply constructs services without any change in their behaviors, it is unlikely that the desired outcome will be achieved, and the organization will be at risk of having SOA be seen as yet another overhyped IT effort that promised to save the world and failed.

Processes

Finally, SOA governance must involve processes for policy creation, communication and education, enforcement, and measurement. It must focus on communication and collaboration first, so it is not seen as a heavy-handed dictatorship. If it is understood and embraced, enforcement will be a simpler task because the staff will want to be compliant, rather than being forced to be compliant. Finally, the effort must be continually measured so that the leaders themselves are held accountable, and changes can be enacted if the desired behaviors are not being achieved.

Is All this Needed?

But why is all of this needed? Aren't we already choosing what applications to build, funding those projects, and designing and deploying those solutions? Before you embark on your SOA journey, there is one critical question that must be asked. Does your organization need to change? If the answer is no, then there's no reason to keep reading. If the answer is yes, based on the fact that you're reading this book, which is probably the case, then you need SOA governance. Simply viewing SOA as a technology-based solution where you choose to use XML, SOAP, and HTTP technologies in place of Enterprise Java Beans, DCOM, CORBA, or any other distributed computing technology is not a change in behavior. Your organization will still be building the same solutions it always has, just with a different set of technologies.

The real challenge behind SOA is not choosing technologies appropriately; it is changing the behavior of the organization so that it can improve. Governance is all about guiding behavior of an organization, so it is understandable that the key to being successful with SOA is governance.

Without SOA governance, the information technology assets of an enterprise are, at best, a collection of independent solutions that are primarily related through proximity. Integration is seen as something to be avoided as much as possible, and where required, is done so as a necessary evil, frequently in a suboptimal manner. With SOA governance, the information technology assets of an enterprise are a collection of interoperating solutions that through effective people, policies, and processes, collectively meet the needs today and of the future for the business organization as a whole.

Summary

In this chapter, we've learned that governance is necessary to ensure that the organization achieves its desired behaviors, whether that organization is a city, a country, a business, or an IT department. This is done through a combination of three things: people, policies, and processes. People are the leaders that are responsible for establishing the desired behavior of the organization, policies are the rules that express the desired behavior, and process ensures that the policies are followed.

We learned that SOA is a new approach where the information technology assets are viewed as a collection of services and consumers. These services and their consumers are expected to operate as a community from day one, rather than being viewed as a collection of individual applications that lack clarity on where capabilities are shared, and have inconsistent internal structures that do not support future change or integration needs.

This shift from application oriented architecture to SOA is a fundamental change to the way that IT operates and likely a change in the way that the business interacts with IT. A change of this scope represents new behaviors, and the way to achieve these desired behaviors is governance.

In the next chapter you will be introduced to the fictional company and its employees that will be used throughout this book and learn about their initial efforts in adopting SOA, and how governance, or the lack thereof, played a role in their successes and their failures.

2

Extending Project Governance for SOA

Every organization's journey to SOA adoption must begin somewhere. Some organizations may take a very top-down approach based upon direction from the Chief Information Officer (CIO) or other senior IT leader, while other organizations may begin with a grass-roots effort from within the IT organization, often times during a single project. This chapter will begin the story of Advasco and describe the beginning of their SOA journey, which falls into the latter. Through their initial experiences you will learn about the role of SOA governance within the typical project governance efforts.

Beginning the SOA Journey

Spencer walked in through the main doors of Advasco, a leading financial conglomerate, on Monday morning knowing it was going to be a busy day. He was part of the Enterprise Architecture team at Advasco, and immediately headed for his weekly meeting with his boss, Elena, the Chief Architect. "Come on in, Spencer," she said. "As you know, we've been given a big challenge over the next few months."

Late last week, the head of the sales and marketing for the insurance division announced that they needed to improve the way they interacted with their customers. Advasco began as a typical financial services company, but had recently expanded into the insurance area through acquisition. They began by acquiring a company that provided homeowner's policies in several Midwest states. Over the next few years, Advasco had acquired several other regional insurance companies. This resulted in an increase in the number of insurance products that it offered, as well as turning Advasco into a nationwide provider. Unfortunately, Advasco was struggling to increase the number of insurance products per customer. Analysis of the situation had determined that while the sales staff of the original organizations had been combined, each of the different insurance products relied on different applications for customer management. As a result, it was far more difficult for the sales agents to know what insurance products any given customer had. After discussing it with Mike, the IT manager supporting insurance products, IT was given the task of providing the sales agents and marketing staff for the insurance division with a single view of the customer.

Elena then said to him, "I had a meeting with Mike to discuss their new initiative to provide a single view of the customer to the sales agents and marketing staff. While he has some great developers in his area, he asked me if Enterprise Architecture could provide some architectural guidance to their effort. Given the excellent integration work you did when Advasco acquired our first company in the insurance area, I think you'd do a great job on this effort."

"It certainly sounds like an exciting project," said Spencer, "I'd love to help out. Just last week, I met with my own insurance agent and saw first hand the frustration he had in trying to see the different insurance products that I have for my family."

"I'm glad to hear that," said Elena, "I'd like you to meet with Mike today and start coming up with an architecture for the effort. I know you've been reading about SOA. Perhaps this effort can serve as a good pilot for some of the techniques."

Spencer agreed. He left Elena's office and went to his desk to set up a meeting with Mike. This was going to be an exciting effort. This initiative was highly visible within the organization, since Advasco's customer approval rating had been taking a beating over the past two years.

In addition, Elena knew that Spencer had been researching SOA. In his reading, he felt that SOA had great potential to change the way that Advasco built applications. This effort would provide an opportunity to try out some of the technologies associated with it.

Later that afternoon, Spencer met with Mike to go through the existing applications. Mike said, "Unfortunately, the situation is a mess. Right now, the application that handles our auto insurance business is completely independent from the application that handles our home insurance business. The same thing is true for the life insurance business. They each have their own databases, requiring our agents to enter all of the customer information in multiple times. It creates a nightmare for our billing department, especially when trying to compute discounts for multiple policy holders. These applications have all been built using different technologies, including COBOL, VB.NET, and Java."

Spencer said, "Well, let's take a managed approach to this effort. Which are the two insurance lines where we most frequently see repeat customers?"

Mike replied, "The most common case is for a customer to hold both an auto insurance policy and a homeowner's policy. It's an easy way to get a multiple policy discount."

"Well, why don't we start with those two systems and see what we can do. I've been reading about SOA and I think it could provide the right approach for this effort."

"I'll trust you on this one Spencer. Elena spoke very highly of you in our meeting last week. As long as you don't think adopting new approaches will impact the timelines, I'm okay with it. The insurance sales and marketing group is under a ton of pressure to get our customer approval rating back up where it should be as quickly as possible."

The next day, Spencer met with the managers responsible for the auto insurance systems and the home insurance systems. Spencer kicked off the meeting, "We're here to discuss how we can make things better for our sales staff. Right now, they have to deal with two separate applications. As a result, sometimes they don't know when they're dealing with someone who is already a customer. Other times, we wind up with inconsistent records across the two systems, or have problems keeping records up-to-date when a customer moves."

Tim, the manager for the auto insurance systems immediately jumped into the conversation, "If we could get the home insurance system to use our customer database, our problems would go away."

Adil, the manager for the home insurance systems, responded to Tim, "We've spent the last 15 years evolving our application and database. It would be much more expensive for us to try to move all our data into your system."

Spencer could sense the tension in the room. Both of these managers had invested many years in their systems, and neither one wanted to relinquish any amount of control. "I don't think consolidating the data will work with the timelines we've been given. What I'd like to do is to create a new customer information service that will provide an abstraction layer in front of both of your databases. You'll both need to modify your applications to use the service rather than going directly to the database, but the service will ensure that both systems remain in sync. In addition, you'll have access to additional information about the customers in each other's systems that you can now incorporate into your applications. Then, at a later time, we can pursue consolidating the databases into a single one. With the service in place, you won't need to make any changes to the front end of your applications when that occurs."

Adil said, "How are you going to make this work? My system leverages a Java front-end talking to our mainframe, while Tim's system is based completely on Microsoft technologies?"

Spencer responded, "I think this a great opportunity to leverage web services technology. It claims to provide interoperability across these platforms, let's give it a try."

Tim said, "Who's going to write this service?"

Spencer suggested, "Since we need to incorporate information from both of your systems, I suggest that we form a team with a developer from each of your groups to design and build the new service."

Adil and Tim agreed, and told Spencer that they would let him know what developers they would contribute to the effort.

Spencer went back to his desk and knew that he had a real challenge on his hands. While the managers involved had committed developers to the effort, he also sensed that there was some hesitancy about the effort. They knew that changes were needed, but it was clear that neither one wanted to give up the control they currently had over their systems. He was hoping that the right developers would get assigned. He knew that many of them had complained about the redundancy that existed across the various applications, but the scope and timeline of their projects prevented them from doing anything about it. This effort was beginning with the right scope, so as long they met timelines, there was a good chance to make it happen.

Over the next few weeks, Spencer's team, including the developers from Adil and Tim's organizations, worked hard to define the new Customer service that both applications would use. The developers were very familiar with the current data models used by each application, and worked together to define the data models and schemas for the new service. While these developers had some knowledge of how the existing applications manipulated the data, they worked solely with each other in defining the functional interface of the service. In the end, the service interface contained some elements of Customer data that was specific to one of the two applications, but they felt that information could be safely ignored by the other application.

The First Milestone

Soon afterwards, Spencer met with Jennifer, the project manager for the auto insurance application, to discuss their schedule. Spencer said, "Hi Jennifer. I wanted to discuss our delivery schedule with you so we can ensure that you can integrate the new Customer service as part of your effort. I know you're making some additional changes to the application besides the migration to the service."

Jennifer took a glance at her project plan and told Spencer, "We're currently planning on going live on October 6th. Our performance tests are planned for September 2nd, and user testing will begin on July 28th."

Spencer said, "Okay, we'll plan on targeting those same dates for our service. Don't hesitate to contact me if you need anything else."

Jennifer didn't. Just two weeks later she sent him an email that said, "Spencer, my developers want to know when they'll have a service they can test against. They've told me that they can't do anymore work until it's available."

Spencer replied, "I'll have one of my developers provide you the URL for our development service right away." He had his team provide it, and didn't hear anything back from Jennifer's team, so he assumed everything was working well. That lasted for about one week when Jennifer came storming into his cubicle.

"What did you do to the service? We were going to demonstrate where we were to one of our users today, and the application crashed when we tried retrieving data," she said. It was clear that it had not been a good morning for her.

"We've been testing the integration with the home insurance data system, and have run into some issues, so our development environment has been up and down all day long as we try to determine what the problem is," he replied.

"Well, you'd better get it fixed soon. I now have a key user who's very nervous about the stability of this new service-based approach, and my developers are simply telling me that they can't do anything about it. I'm going to report this as a serious issue in our Project Management Office (PMO) update on Thursday."

"I'll get right on it, Jennifer. I apologize for this and we'll get it fixed as quickly as we can."

Spencer immediately realized where his mistake was. By giving Jennifer's team the URL for the service in his development environment, he was exposing her application to all of the instability that is normally associated with any development environment. From her perspective, however, she didn't care about his development environment; she needed something that was stable so she could execute her tests and provide demonstrations.

He gathered his developers and told them that they needed to create a stable version of the service that would be separate from their own development efforts that the auto insurance application could use. He suggested that they determine which of their iterations represented a key milestone from the perspective of the auto insurance application. When those iterations were successfully completed, it would be promoted to the stable environment in use by the auto insurance application. They implemented this plan and things got better, at least from Jennifer's perspective.

Unfortunately, Jennifer wasn't the only project manager whose effort was dependent on Spencer's team. Mark was the project manager for the home insurance application, the other consumer of this new service. Like his initial meeting with Jennifer, Spencer met with Mark to find out what his plans were for the home insurance application. Like Jennifer, there were additional changes that Mark was putting into the application in addition to migrating to the new Customer service.

Mark said, "We need to get our application into production by September 15th. There are some new regulations that have been passed, and we need to incorporate them into our application by then or else we can be subject to fines. We plan on beginning active user testing two months before then."

Spencer replied, "Your dates are pretty close to Jennifer's, so I think we'll be okay. We've already set up a stable version of the service for her project, so I'll send the information to you, and your developers can begin testing against it as soon as they'd like."

"That would be great. I know that it's important that we start using your service, so I'm glad that the timelines look good right now. It's very important that our dates are met. I absolutely must deliver no later than September 15th."

The Second Milestone

Spencer passed this information back to his development team and everything was going well until the second milestone release went out. Jennifer's team received the latest interface definition, which included the next set of functionality that her team was going to test. Unfortunately, her developers were not at all happy with the results. Spencer's team had determined the operations to expose in the web service-based solely upon their past knowledge of the applications that would be using it. Unfortunately, some significant changes had occurred to the applications, and their knowledge was out of date. The way in which they had represented the data in the operation was a complete mismatch to the processing model within the auto insurance application. While all the data was there, the way in which the data was organized would require Jennifer's team to completely disassemble the data and reassemble it in the data structures necessary. This had the potential of impacting her team's delivery schedule. Jennifer discussed this with Spencer, and he agreed to modify the service interface according to what her developers needed. This wound up being a relatively simple change for Spencer's team, so it was pushed out as part of the next iteration, two weeks later. That day was no better.

"Spencer, what happened to the service?" Mark said, with a clear sense of irritation in his voice. "We had integrated our application with the last milestone release, and then you go and change all the operations out from underneath us. What gives?"

"Mark, I'm sorry I didn't let you know about those changes. Jennifer, the project manager for the auto insurance upgrade project, wasn't happy with the last milestone release as her developers would have had to do significant rework in order to accommodate the interface design."

"Spencer, what am I supposed to do now? Your changes will now require significant rework in my application to accommodate these new interface changes, and I can't afford any more slips in my schedule."

"Let me set up a meeting with you and Jennifer so we can find an approach that will work with both of your schedules. I'll get it set up for this afternoon," said Spencer.

That afternoon, Spencer met with Mark and Jennifer to discuss the state of affairs. Neither of them was happy about the situation.

"Spencer, I can't take on any more development tasks right now. My team is already struggling to make the necessary changes for these regulatory changes in the time we have left. I can't afford to have them make changes that we didn't need because your team decided to change the service from underneath us," said Mark.

Jennifer replied, "Mark, your project isn't the only one that's important. I've got just as much pressure on me to get this project delivered, and that original interface would have added about three weeks onto my schedule."

Spencer was regretting not having involved Mark and Jennifer's teams back when the original interface design decisions were made. He had trusted that by having developers who had previously worked on both of those applications they would have known what operations would work best for each, but that clearly wasn't the case. While he didn't want to do it, he knew that he had to make sacrifices within his project in order to meet both Mark and Jennifer's needs. He asked, "Mark, if we put the original operations back in the service interface in our next iteration, would that work for you? It would be available within two weeks. Jennifer, we'd leave the new operations in the interface. While I'd like to only provide this functionality in one way, I realize that in order to meet both of your schedules, this is the only way that can be done."

Mark and Jennifer thought about this option, and they both agreed that they could make this work. All three of them agreed to continue meeting on a regular basis to ensure that there would be no more surprises throughout the rest of the effort. Spencer left the meeting very relieved that he was able to find an approach that would work. He knew that his experience was stronger on the technical side of things, and didn't realize that the far bigger challenges would lie in the coordination and communication efforts.

The Opportunity

Over the next three months things went well for these three projects. Spencer, Jennifer, and Mark all met regularly and ensured that any issues that arose were dealt with to the satisfaction of everyone involved. In one of these conversations, Spencer found out that a new project had just been spun up from the annuity department. Even though this project was outside of the original plans, Spencer thought it would be an easy conversation given the success he'd had with Jennifer and Mark. He arranged for a meeting with the project manager, Ryan.

"Hi Ryan, Thanks for agreeing to meet with me. I'm the solution architect for the new Customer service project. The auto insurance team and the home insurance team are both leveraging it, and I thought it might be something you would be interested in. By utilizing it, you'll be well-positioned for providing visibility into the other products that annuity customers have."

Ryan replied, "I've heard a little bit about your effort, Spencer. Is it currently in production?"

Spencer responded, "We're scheduled to go live on September 15th along with the new home insurance system."

Ryan said, "Why don't you send some information about your service to my solution architect, Ramesh?"

"I'll do that," said Spencer. Spencer had worked with Ramesh on a previous project, so he decided to talk to him right away. Spencer walked down to Ramesh's desk, "Hey Ramesh, I just met with your project manager, Ryan. I'm working on a new Customer service project and I thought your annuity system could leverage it."

He went on to give Ramesh the details on the service that was being built, and how it was providing an abstraction layer for the auto insurance and home insurance customer databases, and positioning them for consolidation which would save the company significant costs, in addition to allowing them to gain the visibility they needed to start selling other products to existing customers.

Ramesh said, "This looks really promising, but who's going to take care of putting our database behind your abstraction layer?"

"Our efforts are nearly completed for the home and auto applications. My team has some extra cycles available, and from what I understand, your database is reasonably consistent with the home system, unlike some of the others."

"Well, if you're offering some free resources for the project, I'll at least take a look at your service documentation and meet with Ryan."

Spencer said, "Great! Just let me know if there's anything you need."

A week went by, and Spencer had not heard anything back from Ramesh, so he went to see him again. "Ramesh, did you get a chance to talk to Ryan?"

"Oh! Hi Spencer, sorry I didn't get back to you. I've been busy trying to keep things on track. I did get a chance to talk to Ryan, but he was concerned about taking on the additional scope of moving away from their existing database to the new service."

"Did you tell him that we'll take care of the work necessary within the service to add your database?"

"Trust me, I did. After looking at your documentation, it really didn't look like it would be much work at all for us to integrate in your new service, but he didn't want to hear any of it. Not only was he concerned about the added scope, he also said that he didn't want his project to be dependent on some other team. He said he'd done that in the past, and it only led to delays, angry meetings, and some poor performance reviews for everyone involved."

Spencer decided to go and speak directly to Ryan. While Ramesh indicated that he had talked to Ryan, Spencer still wasn't sure whether he had done a good job in hitting the key selling points for using the service. Spencer was very passionate about SOA, and realized that not everyone shared that same passion. He caught up with Ryan the next day.

"I spoke with Ramesh yesterday, and he said that you told him not to pursue leveraging the service from my team. Is there something I can do that might change your mind?"

"Spencer, I'm sorry, but I just can't take on any additional scope in this project. I appreciate the offer, and the fact that your team was willing to take on the work to integrate our database, but I've had too many bad experiences in the past with creating dependencies on teams outside of my control."

"I really think this service would position you well for the future, since you know that Advasco is really trying to improve our relationship with our customers.

Jennifer and Mark are both in the same situation, and we've been able to deliver everything they've needed without impacting their schedule. Would it help if you talked to them?"

"I really don't have time for this Spencer. Jennifer and Mark were both mandated to use this service thing that you're so excited about, and I know both of them were pretty nervous about it. I am under no such mandate, and I'm not going to take on any risk that I don't have to. Now, if you'll excuse me, I've got a project to manage."

Humbled, Spencer went back to his cube looking like a dog with its tail between its legs. He was frustrated that even though the solution architect for the project had reviewed the service documentation and told Ryan that it wouldn't impact on the project, Ryan refused to budge. Not even the impact of the company's desire to improve its relationship with its customers could change his mind.

Spencer went home that night and talked with his wife, Alexandra, about his day. "I just don't understand why I couldn't convince Ryan to leverage the service. I tried to remove every road block that I could think of, and he still just said 'No' without even looking into the details."

Alexandra responded, "While I know you believe strongly in this, you really were asking him to step outside of his comfort zone. Like he said, Jennifer and Mark didn't have a choice. They were told up front that they had to use your service, so they planned for it from the beginning. From my experience, a project manager's worst nightmare is having dependencies that are outside of his control, and that's exactly what you were asking him to do. I think most of the project managers I know would have said 'No' as well. As much as this may have helped Advasco in the future, I think you need to focus on ensuring that your efforts for Mark and Jennifer are successful. Nothing breeds interest like success."

Spencer thought about what she said and agreed, "I can see your point. I shouldn't think that the whole thing is going to fall apart just because of one project manager. Mark and Jennifer have been very happy for the past two months after our early problems."

The service development effort continued, and on September 8th, a week ahead of schedule, the service went live along with Mark's application. Four weeks later, on October 6th, Jennifer's application was added to the list.

Beginning Your SOA Journey

Many organizations start their journey towards SOA through some sort of grass roots effort. Unfortunately, these efforts normally result in what's known as **JBOS (Just a Bunch of Services)**. Typically, a project that had previously used some form of distributed component technology, such as Enterprise Java Beans, has now chosen to use XML or SOAP and HTTP, instead. The issue with this approach is that the service boundary that establishes the consumer and provider relationship really doesn't exist when one team is responsible for both the consumer and the provider.

Eventually, the organization will encounter a situation where the development of the service and development of the consumer takes place in a separate project. This could be due to there being more than one consumer, a B2B scenario where services are developed for consumption by partner companies, a large program that involves many independently managed projects, or simply a decision that the organization makes as it learns more about SOA. In our example, this was exactly the case. There was a program that encompassed three separate projects, two that involved development of service consumers, and one that handled the service development. The two consumers were the front-end for the auto insurance system and the front-end for the home insurance system. Spencer's project was responsible for creating a new service that provided an abstraction layer in front of the data systems for both applications.

Key Project Roles

The nice thing about projects and programs is that they have an explicit hierarchy. If a developer has a question or concern, they work with the project architect. The project architect may take things to the project manager, and the project manager may take things to the sponsor. If it's a program, then there's likely a hierarchy of architects and project managers, but everything bubbles its way up to the top. Everyone working on the project understands the objectives, the scope, the milestones, and the deadlines. This explicit hierarchy is the first, and often only, source of governance within the project. Within the project we have one piece of the governance puzzle: **people**. The challenge, however, is that the people only have authority within the project. If your SOA adoption efforts are broader than that single project or program, you'll likely run into problems.

In our Advasco example, Spencer ran into exactly this problem. Initially, Spencer only had to deal with project managers that were within the overall program. These project managers knew that the desired outcome was a shared, accurate, complete view of the customer, and it would be achieved through usage of the new service. As a result, they worked together with Spencer to ensure that outcome would be reached. When Spencer went outside of the program, however, his position of authority did not go with him. When he met with Ryan, he had no perceived or explicit authority. Even though the company had recognized a need to improve its image with its customers, the scope of that effort within IT was limited to the home and auto insurance areas. Therefore, for Ryan, service reuse was not on his list of desired outcomes, and regardless of how good Spencer made it sound, it was not something that he was willing to risk for the outcomes that he did desire.

The Service Contract

In this example, we clearly had a service provider, Spencer and his team, and two service consumers, the auto insurance application whose development efforts were managed by Jennifer and the home insurance application managed by Mark. A key aspect of this example is that these three efforts were independently managed, even though all being under a common program. A service should be independent of all consumers and this begins at the time that version one is developed, not at the time version one goes into production. In our example, imagine if the service development was under the management of either Mark's project or Jennifer's project. If a conflict arose, whose project would win out? Clearly, the project manager that oversees the service development effort has the upper hand, and will likely make decisions that will benefit their own project first. By separating out the service development as an independently managed effort, both of the two consumers are now equal, as they should be.

When we have the notion of a service consumer and a service provider, we need an explicit representation of the relationship between them, and that relationship is a service contract. This is no different than how we deal with services in the real world. If you hire a crew to replace the roof on your home, the first step is for you and the construction crew to sign a contract that governs the work. It provides governance by establishing policies. These include the hours that work will take place, the time in which the work will be done, the payment schedule and conditions, the behavior of the crew in the event of bad weather, and so on. In the world of SOA, the service contract is the collection of policies that govern the interaction between a service consumer and a service provider. That contract states the messages that will be exchanged, the URIs to be utilized, and more. We will continue to fill in details of the service contract throughout the rest of the book.

In this chapter, the initial focus was on two factors: the functional interface and the delivery schedule of the implementation. This is where most organizations start as the functional interface and a working implementation of that interface are clearly the minimum mandatory elements. It is no surprise that terminology like **contract-first** quickly sprung up as the varying technical approaches started to gain in popularity.

This chapter also addressed another key element of service contracts. In the real world, a contract is a binding agreement between two parties. Using our earlier roofing example, if the contractor replaces the roof on your house as well as the roof on your neighbor's house, he would have one contract with you and one contract with your neighbor. While you and your neighbor are both receiving the same service (a new roof) the terms and conditions around that service are likely to be different. You may both have been presented a standard contract to begin with, but from that point on, each one of you may have made your own adjustments or additions. The same approach needs to hold true for technology services. You may choose to expose a subset of operations to one consumer, while another consumer may have access to all operations.

In our example, Spencer's efforts initially fell short. He had initial conversations with Jennifer, but the only thing that came out of it was some agreement on when things had to go live. There was no discussion of the service interface, no discussion of the delivery schedule of milestone releases, or anything else. Given that this service was only going to be consumed internally, the development of the interface should have been a joint effort of both the consumer and provider. Spencer's team would bring domain knowledge from the provider's side, Jennifer's team would bring domain knowledge from the consumer's side, and together they would establish a service interface that was amenable to both. Instead, Spencer's team developed the initial service interface in a vacuum, creating something that may have met their needs, but did not meet the needs of the consumer. Meeting the needs of the consumer is the most important aspect of providing a service.

The second mistake that Spencer made was that he did not establish a formal definition of the handoffs that would be required between his team and Jennifer's team. In providing Jennifer's team an endpoint that could be used during development, he thought he was doing the right thing, but then when that endpoint changed out from underneath them, since, after all, it was under development, it had an impact on the trust between Jennifer's team and his team.

This particular situation can be a challenging one for many organizations, because the basic design of their environments often assumes that everything required for a project is under the control of the project team, and can therefore be promoted through the environments in lock-step. Now, when service consumers and the service provider are being developed according to their own timelines, instability can be introduced.

The appropriate way to handle this situation is to make explicit those policies that govern the interaction between the service consumers and the service provider during the design and development phase, rather than dealing with situations that arise on an ad hoc basis. The service provider has the responsibility for delivering a stable version of the service at various points throughout the project, and deploying it onto a stable platform that only changes according to the policies within the contracts enacted with the consumer teams.

For example, suppose both the service consumer and service provider are taking an iterative approach to the development of their solutions. In order to allow the service consumer adequate time for testing and feedback, the service provider may only promote a subset of their iteration builds to an integration environment for use by the service consumer. The service consumer would be required to provide feedback within a specified amount of time in order to have the fix included in a subsequent integration release. This is shown in the following figure:

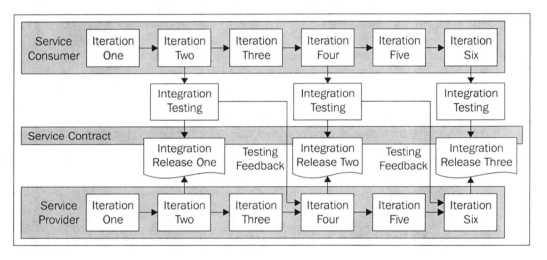

In short, within a single project, iterative, agile development can certainly take precedence. Across projects, however, the handoffs should be formalized and explicitly specified as part of the service contract, especially when two or more consumers are involved.

Adding SOA to Traditional Project Governance

While the big change for the organization is learning how to manage the consumer-provider relationship, we can't forget about traditional project governance. Today, your organization may make use of architecture reviews, design reviews, code reviews, and operational readiness reviews as part of the software development process. These reviews already embody the three components of governance: people, policies, and process. These reviews more than likely involve resources from outside the project that the enterprise has positioned as authorities. An architecture review may involve enterprise architects, more senior architects, or other architectural peers. A design review may involve architects or senior developers. A code review may involve senior developer or other development peers. The operational readiness review probably involves members of the operational areas to ensure that a handoff to the support teams will be successful.

In order for these reviews to be successful, the policies that need to be followed for architecture, design, coding, and deployment need to be known to the project team. In the absence of documented policies that encourage the desired behavior, these reviews tend to be a show of power by the review team, where it is simply an exercise in trying to find something about the project to make the statement that they know better than the project team. Meanwhile, the project team plays a guessing game trying to determine what the review team wants to see, usually winding up wrong. In short, without documented policies, the review tends to be a lose-lose situation for all involved.

The process is the part that can vary. Some organizations choose to utilize a formal review process where an hour or two of time is scheduled with the reviewing body, the team prepares a formal presentation, and the review takes place. However, it doesn't need to be this heavyweight. Any of these reviews could also be done in a more informal manner, with a single meeting between a recognized authority for the review being done and the project architect or technical lead. If there is a formal technical hierarchy in the organization, the process may simply be part of the normal conversation that a project architect has with their architecture manager on a regular basis. Finally, an organization can even choose to have no review process, and simply trust that the decision makers on the project have awareness of the policies that must be followed.

So how does SOA change the current governance model for projects? Presuming your existing governance model is working, the only thing that SOA introduces is additional policies. If your existing governance model isn't working, which is a subject for another book, consider making a change.

You now have a project that is building a new artifact, the service. While we discussed the importance of involving potential consumers in the definition of the service interface, the enterprise also has a role. Policies that are normally enforced by an external review board are typically associated with ensuring consistency across projects. When building services, the areas for consistency are:

- The technologies used for the service implementation
- The technologies used for communication between the consumer and the provider
- The representation of the information that is transferred between the consumers and the provider

Service Implementation Technologies

The first area that an enterprise may strive for consistency is in the technologies used to build services, also known as service platform technologies. There's a good chance that an organization may already have some standardization in this area, such as a single Java EE application server. Even if they do, there is still room for standardization.

At a minimum, the organization will need a general purpose application server and an associated development framework, such as a Java EE application server or Windows Server and the Microsoft .NET framework. Both of these platforms provide libraries for many different types of service communication technologies, as well as a robust library of open-source frameworks either as alternative or as extensions for other purposes. Depending on your organization, you may have one or many of these platforms. A general principle that organizations try to use is to not have two tools for the same job. That being said, if an organization has a federated IT department, whether due to past acquisitions, geographic needs, or other reasons, each of these separate IT groups may have their own standards.

In addition to the general purpose application server, another common service platform is the automated process platform, frequently associated with the use of BPEL technologies. This is a new breed of development platform tailored towards the orchestration of other services. Typically, it involves a graphical modeler, providing a drag-and-drop metaphor for connecting services in an orchestrated sequence, such as shown in the following figure:

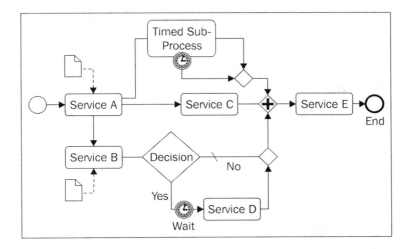

Depending on the product chosen, it may include some out-of-the-box adapters for doing common activities, such as retrieving records from a relational database, publishing messages to an enterprise messaging systems, or sending an email message.

The recommended approach for determining the appropriate number of service platforms is to first determine the service types that an organization may need to provide. A service type is a class of service with a specific set of capabilities that may lend itself to specific technologies. Common types for which you may consider having specific platforms include:

- Composite services
- Automated (Orchestrated) processes
- Integration services
- Presentation services
- Management services
- Information services
- Content subscription services
- General business services

Composite services are, as the name implies, services that are built from other services. This typically involves combining the output of several services and combining it to be delivered to a consumer through a single service.

Automated processes, as was discussed earlier, are about the orchestration of a collection of services to perform a higher level function. Frequently, composite services can be thought of as a subset of the overall space of automated processes.

Integration services are services that are geared towards communication with third-party systems, such as SAP and Oracle. These are frequently associated with **Enterprise Application Integration**, or **EAI**, technologies. While EAI, as a category, has lost favor, there is still plenty of need for integration technologies in communicating with these complex application platforms.

Presentation services are services that provide user interface functionality, whether simply content in a presentation-friendly format, or fully featured presentation components suitable for composition in a portal context.

Management services are services that are geared towards the management of IT systems, typically leveraging technologies like **SNMP (Simple Network Management Protocol)** and **JMX (Java Management Extensions)** for communication.

Information services are services that are intended for data access and manipulation. These are typically marketed as Data Service Platforms or Enterprise Information Integration products.

Content subscription services, such as news feeds, are intended to provide content to consumers on a subscription basis using technologies such as **RSS (Really Simple Syndication)** and Atom.

General business services is the final service type, and is intended to be the catch-all for other services that don't cleanly fit into any of the previous categories. These would normally be implemented using a general purpose application server platform.

Service Communication Technologies

The next set of technologies that an organization may standardize on is service communication technologies. While much has been written on how adopting web services is not the same as adopting SOA, one or more technologies must still be chosen for service communication. This may vary by the service type involved. While in the past, organizations may have leveraged distributed component technologies such as CORBA or Enterprise Java Beans, today most organizations are leveraging either Web Services technologies, some less-restrictive form rooted in XML and HTTP (also known as **POX—Plain Old XML**), or REST.

In the past, a very important aspect of choosing a communication technology was interoperability. Most distributed communication technologies were platform-specific, focused on communication within a platform rather than across platforms. This posed a significant problem when an enterprise had multiple platforms in the environment, which today is the norm for any large organization. This is a challenge that is still being fought today, with each technology getting closer and closer to achieving out-of-the-box interoperability in a very heterogeneous environment.

WS-I Compliance

In the case of web services, there is an industry organization whose specific charter is to establish best practices for **WS-I (Web Services Interoperability)**. As of 2008, there are well over 60 specifications that are related to web services, so determining the right way for using each of them can be a challenging exercise. WS-I has defined a series of profiles (starting with the Basic Profile) that provide best practices for how to use various subsets of the web services specifications. As a best practice on its own, if you choose to leverage web services technologies as part of your technology portfolio for SOA adoption, you should ensure that all platforms involved are compliant with the WS-I Basic Profile.

Security Credentials

Another factor that must be considered when choosing service communication technologies is security. At the time of writing, security is still a large differentiator between some of the popular approaches today, and also a source of potential interoperability problems, even when there are no functional interoperability issues. For example, within web services, the WS-Security specification defines a framework for placing security tokens within a SOAP message. Building on that framework, there are now several standard profiles for common security tokens, including a basic username and password combination, X.509 certificates, **SAML (Security Assertion Markup Language)** assertions, and Kerberos tickets. So, while two parties may both support web services, if a provider decides to only accept security tokens via the Kerberos profile, while the consumer is only capable of sending SAML assertions, we still may have interoperability issues.

Overall, organizations are in a far better state with the options available to them now than ten years ago. While there are still interoperability challenges, most of them can be overcome through a variety of means. The role of governance in this is to ensure that communication technologies are used consistently and appropriately, not to ensure that the organization only chooses one communication technology.

Service Interface Specification

Perhaps the most important aspect of enterprise governance on service technologies is in the interface specification. Regardless of whether an organization leverages web services, REST, XML over HTTP, Enterprise Java Beans, or virtually any other communication technology, information needs to be transferred between a service consumer and a service provider. While choosing a single communication technology can resolve interoperability problems when transferring information between a single consumer and single provider, there is still risk for inconsistency in the information when a service consumer talks with multiple service providers.

In our example, Spencer had the challenge of providing a Customer service that met the needs of both the auto insurance system and the home insurance system. This proved to be a challenge because each of these systems had their own definition of what a Customer is. In designing the original interface, Spencer's team focused inward, basing their decisions on the service development team's understanding of the service implementation. The path of least resistance for this team was to simply base the service interface on that knowledge, working with people within their own project. In other words, the implementation model of the information bubbled its way out to the service interface as shown in the following figure:

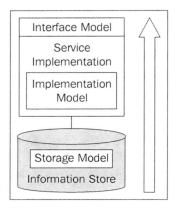

This is a bottom-up approach, where the representation of the information begins with how it is stored in the information store (for example, relational database) and is expressed in a storage model. The information is used within the service implementation in some form, that representation is known as the implementation model. Finally, that information is exposed via the service interface, as the interface model. The challenge that is faced is that the easiest path for a development team is to simply let these models bubble up. It took many years for the industry to realize that a model that was well-suited for storing information (for example, a relational

data model) may not be well-suited for processing information, and thus a new model was needed (for example, an object model). Likewise, it is also true that the implementation model is not well-suited for transmitting information to another processing node, because their processing needs (and possibly their platform for implementation) is going to be different.

An alternative approach is to take a very consumer-oriented view. Instead of allowing the internal service implementation to drive the interface model, the model is determined through analysis of the service consumers, as shown in the following figure:

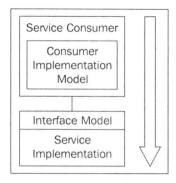

At first glance, this may seem like the more service-oriented way of approaching the interface design, since after all, services are about consumption. Unfortunately, not all consumers are created equal. In our example, Spencer had a challenge in meeting the needs of both Mark's team and Jennifer's team because each of them had their own model, and there were inconsistencies between them.

An approach that Spencer could have taken would have been to have his team meet with Mark's team and Jennifer's team to balance each of their respective interests in coming up with a service interface in which all parties agree. While this may have prevented some of Spencer's problems, it still is not without its challenges. Suppose that a few months later, Advasco chooses to partner with a new company for billing services. Clearly, these billing services need Customer information, but it is likely that the new company has their own definition of what a Customer is. So, the situation we now have is shown in the following figure:

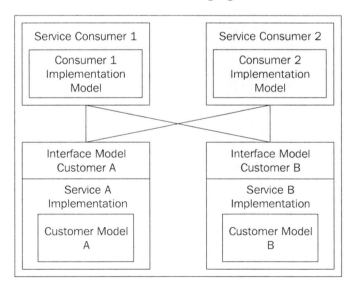

In this situation, we have two service consumers, 1 and 2, and two service providers, A and B. Both services A and B require some representation of Customer information as part of their service interface. Unfortunately, if these representations are inconsistent, the burden of transforming and mapping between them fall back to each individual consumer. Every consumer that needs to use both services A and B winds up having to implement that transformation and mapping within their own code. As the number of services that a particular consumer interacts with grows, the situation gets more and more complicated.

Using a Canonical Model

The approach to solving this dilemma is to embrace the notion of a canonical model. A canonical model is an information model that is independent from any particular service consumer or service provider. When adopting a canonical model, service interfaces are defined according to it. In this way, a consumer or a provider only needs to know how to map to the canonical model, rather than having to know how to map to any of the possible interface models of the independent service providers. The picture now looks like this:

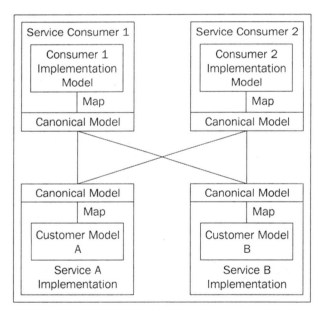

The hidden challenge behind this approach is the actual development of the canonical model itself. Performing an analysis of all possible consumers and all possible providers that deal with a particular piece of information, and then trying to find common ground across all of them can be a painful and time-consuming exercise. Many organizations choose to avoid this altogether and base their canonical model on an industry standard for their line of business. In some cases, this is exactly the right thing to do, especially if the services being designed are going to be exposed externally.

While the construction of a canonical model is beyond the scope of this book, there is no doubt that there is a need for an information model independent of any consumer or provider that establishes policies for message interfaces. In the absence of such a model, the path of least resistance is to push the implementation models of individual consumers or provider out into service interfaces, which leads to a far worse situation of point-to-point integrations, and many-to-many mappings between them, contained within each service consumer. At the same time, if the development of an enterprise model is a painful and time-consuming process that frequently ends in failure, what is an organization to do?

To establish some best practices, we must remember that the goal of governance here is to ensure consistency among service interface definitions, not to ensure that the enterprise creates a canonical model. Consistency can be achieved following these best practices:

- **Consult all potential service consumers**: In our example, Spencer eventually consulted the two consumers that were associated with his program, but as we found out later in the chapter, there were other potential customers, such as Ryan, as well. Some human judgment is always needed, as a project can quickly get into analysis paralysis.

- **Consult service owners that also use similar information**: In addition to consulting potential service consumers, you should also contact other service providers that may also utilize the same information. With good use of a registry or repository tool, other service providers should be easily found.

- **In the absence of an existing standard, leverage an industry standard if one exists**: Many times, groups with vested interests have a difficult time reaching consensus and as a result, they bring in a professional mediator. In the case of service interfaces, an industry standard can act as the external mediator, providing a model that is independent of any of the models at hand, yet having the backing of an industry coalition that focuses in the particular domain at hand.

- **If the services are going to be exposed externally, leverage an industry standard if one exists**: It is difficult enough to get internal groups to agree on messaging standards, doing so with other organizations can be even more of a challenge. If an organization pushes its own model on its partners, it can be perceived as domineering. It also runs the risk of alienating partners if other competitors offer similar services based on standards. If a standard exists, it should be leveraged. If one doesn't exist, an organization should think carefully about driving a process to establish one rather than trying to make their own model the de facto standard.

- **Define your plan for change**: Regardless of how many potential consumers and providers are consulted, it is likely that, at some point in the future, your interface will change. Rather than starting with the assumption that your interface will be defined once and never be modified, start with the assumption that it will change, and walk through the steps necessary to ensure that the change happens in a smoothly managed fashion. Decide how existing consumers will be notified, how long previous versions will be supported, and at what timeframes the new interfaces will get rolled out. We discussed how the service contract needs to explicitly specify the interactions between service consumer and service provider during service development, but it must also specify the interactions that will occur after the development of the initial version, including the development of subsequent versions.

Web Services, POX over HTTP, and REST

Any conversation about service interface technologies would not be complete without a discussion about the differences between the three most popular interface technologies today, which are web services, POX over HTTP, and REST. We've mentioned web services quite a bit in this chapter, so let's begin there. Web services provide the most explicit service interface of the three approaches, through the use of a **WSDL (Web Services Description Language)** file. The WSDL file describes how to interact with a service by specifying the URLs to which messages should be directed, as well as schemas for the messages themselves, using XML Schema. A service is comprised of one or more operations, and each operation can specify messages associated with its usage including a request message, a response message, and fault messages. At least from a functional perspective, the message formats are very explicit.

POX over HTTP is more of a descriptor than it is a standard. In short, it leverages HTTP with XML messages as the payload on requests and responses, but there are no explicit interface definitions whatsoever. Consumers are completely reliant on word of mouth or published documentation to determine what the allowed XML messages are. It can be thought of as web services without the WSDL, SOAP, and WS-*. It is certainly very common to find it used in AJAX applications where a web browser uses JavaScript to send and receive XML messages with a back-end system.

REST, which many people mistakenly confuse with POX, stands for **Representational State Transfer**, and is based on the work of Dr. Roy Fielding. REST views the world not as a collection of services, but rather a collection of resources. Each resource is uniquely addressable via a URI, and all resources can be interacted with according to a universal interface. When using it with HTTP, the universal interface is generally accepted as the HTTP operation of POST, GET, PUT, and DELETE. When using REST, a query for information would always be done via a HTTP GET operation, while when using POX over HTTP, it may be tunneled through HTTP POST, and when using Web Services, it is most certainly tunneled through HTTP POST. The key difference for this discussion, however, is that REST does not make the information model explicitly known at design time via the use of an interface specification, like a WSDL file.

Between these three approaches, the single biggest differentiator from the point of view of interface technologies is the use of an explicit interface definition that includes an information model with Web Services and the distinct absence of one for either POX or REST. The one common truth, however, is that all three of these technologies can be used to share information between systems. If the information being shared is done so using different representations, it places more complexity with the consumer to deal with those inconsistencies. Regardless of whether the information model is explicitly specified or not, there is still a role for governance in ensuring that appropriate consistency is maintained and the associated complexity in maintaining that consistency is appropriately managed.

Summary

In this chapter, we walked through a simple example of a company's initial SOA efforts. We saw how project and program structure establishes a recognized set of authorities within the project or program, but how that authority does not go beyond the project or program. We saw how working across project boundaries, even when under a common program, can be challenging when the required interactions are not made explicit. We saw the challenge that a service provider faces when trying to establish an interface that meets the needs of multiple consumers, both from a functional standpoint as well as a scheduling standpoint.

Beyond project governance, the role of enterprise governance was introduced and how the desired behavior for the organization is consistency. While a single standard is one way of achieving consistency, it is not the only way, nor may it be the right way, depending on the structure of your organization. Adopting SOA does not establish the need for enterprise governance; it simply inserts new policies into the mix of things that must be governed. The three key policy areas are service implementation technologies, which are the platforms and frameworks used to build services, service communication technologies, which are the technologies used to allow communication between service consumers and service providers, and service interface technologies, which are the information models that are used within service messages. Of these three, service interface technologies pose the most challenging problem, as inconsistent information models create point-to-point integration scenarios and increase the amount of complexity in service consumers. Adopting a canonical information model, or allowing one to grow organically, can manage this complexity effectively.

Avoiding a Bunch of Services

3

How does an organization move from simply creating services that have value within a single project to services that have value within the enterprise? If they don't, they won't have a SOA; they'll simply have a bunch of services. This chapter will demonstrate the steps that Advasco took to avoid that situation.

Undirected Service Creation

By the start of the year, the successes of the new Customer Information Service were beginning to roll in. The field agents that were using the new auto and home insurance applications were very pleased that they now could easily see which customers held multiple policies, and which ones did not. In turn, the customers were more satisfied that they were being presented with possible discounts without having to ask, and the customers that held both auto and home insurance policies were treated with the appropriate respect due a repeat customer.

Andrea, the CIO, called Elena into her office, "Elena, I wanted to thank you for your team's work on the effort associated with the auto and home insurance applications. While I know it's still early, the feedback we've received from the field agents has been great."

Elena replied, "Thank you very much. I know Spencer and the project team put a lot of hard work into the effort. Spencer has been looking for opportunities to apply some of what he has learned about SOA, and it's great that his initial effort has been a success so far."

"You know, I've also been hearing from colleagues that they're looking to embrace SOA as well. In my next Town Hall, I'm definitely going to give some praise to the efforts and encourage others to incorporate SOA into their projects."

"I'm sure Spencer will be happy to hear that. Let me know if there's anything you need from me or my team in preparation for it."

"I'll do that. Once again, thanks for the excellent work. I'll be sure to stop by and see Spencer and his team and thank them for their effort directly."

Andrea did exactly that, and Spencer appreciated the gesture. He came home that night and told Alexandra about the result. "The CIO personally came by today to thank me for my efforts on the new Customer Information Service. She was very excited about the results and told me she's going to include SOA adoption as part of her message to all of IT in her next Town Hall."

"That's great news," said Alexandra, "I know you've really been putting in a lot of time to learn about SOA and it's great that all of your hard work will pay off."

At the next IT Town Hall, Andrea was true to her word. After giving her review of recent projects, which did include the updates to the auto and home insurance systems, but surprisingly made no mention of the new customer service, Andrea spoke about some of the new and emerging topics in technology that she felt were important to the future success of IT. In these topics, she included SOA. With this one, she said, "We've had some initial success with SOA, and I believe that we can have more. I encourage all of you to leverage it on your projects."

Afterwards, Spencer was walking back to his cubicle with Elena, discussing the talk. "It was great that Andrea mentioned SOA. Hopefully, we'll start building on the progress that's been made so far."

Elena replied, "Yes, it never hurts to have the CIO mention something you're interested in seeing applied."

Over the next few months, just as Andrea had recommended, several projects did exactly that, and tried to embrace services. Much to the surprise of Andrea, Elena, and Spencer, however, the success stories were not flowing freely. In fact, it seemed that the tap was completely shut off.

Effort One: Hot Potato

One of the first efforts that had a lot of promise was a set of three different projects that had all identified a common need for an address validation service. One was a project associated with account maintenance, one was a system that was going to pre-qualify applicants for insurance, and the final one was for the facilities organization that dealt with all of the real estate associated with their branch offices. The first project to get underway was for the account maintenance area. Maria was the project manager for this effort, and she was having lunch with a few of the other project managers. They were talking about their latest assignments, and Maria mentioned that she was now working on the account maintenance project and that her technical lead recommended that they try to leverage SOA. One of the services they thought they needed was for customer address validation.

One of the other project managers, Beth, said, "You know, I'm working on the facilities management project and I think we're going to need something that will do that as well."

Another project manager, Jim, also said, "Hey, I think my project could use that service, too." They agreed to get together back at work and discuss their joint needs.

At that meeting, the conversation began with Jim and Beth both asking Maria, "So when can you deliver that service to us?"

Maria responded, "When was the decision made that my project would deliver this? Jim, your project is the one that will likely be taking in the most new addresses, shouldn't your project be the one to handle this? Do you think my project will deliver this?"

Jim said, "But my project has to be in place by July 15th. My users will throw a fit if we don't deliver by then. I can't afford to add time in my schedule to accommodate the needs of your projects."

At this point, Beth began to get a bit frustrated, "Look, I don't care which one of your projects provides the service, but if you expect me to use it, I have to have something to start coding against within two weeks."

Unfortunately, nothing was resolved at this meeting. In fact, the teams continued each on their own way until Elena met with each of the solution architects and found out that no agreement was ever reached on who would develop the service. Elena gathered the three project managers from these projects, along with Spencer, for a meeting and put down an ultimatum. "I recently met with all three of the solution architects responsible for your projects and it is my understanding that even though they all agree that sharing a single address validation service would be the best course, they're presently all on a course to build their own. That's simply unacceptable. There's no good reason for all of these projects to be expending the effort to build their own implementation. From what I learned, the sole reason that this happened is that you couldn't agree on who would take responsibility for building it."

Immediately, Beth jumped in, "I told both of them that it didn't matter to me which one of them wrote the service, I just needed something right away. As a result, I had to have my developers start working on it if I wanted to meet my dates."

Jim countered, "Beth, if you needed something so quickly, why didn't you volunteer to write the service and let us use it?"

Elena knew she needed to pacify the situation, "We're not here to dwell on how we got to this place. We're here to figure out how to get back on the right path. That path is the creation of a single service that all three of your projects will use. Spencer, you've got the most knowledge around SOA of anyone here. Do you have any recommendations?"

Spencer said, "Actually I do. One of the reasons for building services is to define boundaries where things can change independently. One of the ways to determine which team should have ownership over the service is to figure out which application space, over time, is the most likely to be the source of change. If the other applications are merely along for the ride, then it probably doesn't make much sense for them to take ownership of the service. Maria, doesn't your team monitor the postal regulations?"

Maria replied, "Yes, we do, and they change almost every year."

Spencer then said, "Jim, how does your team normally handle these changes?"

Jim hesitantly replied, "Well, we normally don't, and when we encounter a question about them, we usually go talk to someone in Maria's area."

As he watched the realization sink in, Spencer said, "Do you see my point? It's most likely that Maria's area is going to be the one that would be tracking the changes that would result in a change to the service."

Maria responded, "I see your point. In addition to the postal regulations, my organization is responsible for all of the non-position related account information. We handle all of the address change notifications, and deal with returned mail. I'm pretty sure that if anything ever needed to change about address verification, my group would be the first one to know."

Beth and Jim agreed. They both indicated that they really only cared about whether an address was valid or not.

Spencer said, "Well, it looks like we have a winner."

Elena told Maria to immediately work with Beth and Jim to come up with a service interface that worked for all, and get back on the path of having a single implementation. The managers from the organizations weren't very happy about the schedule impact that all of the projects took as a result, but they knew that Andrea had made SOA a goal, and as a result, they went along with the changes.

Effort Two: What Customer Service?

The next project that didn't go as expected was an application from the brokerage business. This application was a new portfolio management system, allowing both financial consultant and customer to have access to portfolio management and proposal capabilities. As part of the design of this solution, the team determined that one of the services they needed was a Customer Information Service.

Unfortunately, this team had no knowledge whatsoever of the Customer Information Service that had already been built by Spencer's team. As a result, they went ahead and developed their own Customer Information Service, rather than leveraging the work that had already been performed previously.

As part of the operational readiness review, Elena looked over the operational support manual, and noticed that the document made reference to a Customer Information Service. She assumed it was the same one that Spencer's team had created. She saw Spencer in the hallway and said, "Hey Spencer, I see that your Customer Information Service has another customer from the financial services area."

Spencer replied, "What? That's the first I've ever heard about anything from the financial services area. Are you sure?"

Elena said, "I was just reviewing an operational readiness document from them and I saw a reference to a Customer Information Service, and I assumed it was yours. I'd better go take a deeper look."

Elena returned to her desk and read more into the document and had her fears validated. The project had created a new Customer Information Service. She went and found the project architect and asked him, "Why did you create a brand new Customer Information Service? Didn't you know that we already had one that was built by Spencer and his team for the auto and home insurance lines? I'm sure he could have easily extended it to support your needs."

The architect replied, "I had no idea that there already was a Customer Information Service. I normally don't have any interaction with the insurance areas, so I don't know how I would have found out about it. I would have been happy to leverage it. I thought we were doing the right thing by breaking out this service and building it."

Elena was now beginning to see that this SOA journey was not going to be an easy one.

Effort Three: Where Did They Go?

Finally, back in the insurance department where the SOA effort initially began, the home insurance team was in need of a service that would validate whether the company was allowed to sell certain products in a particular state. Advasco was continually trying to expand operations, so the answer to this question changed on a frequent basis. The team was aware that the auto insurance team had recently completed a similar service and thought that it could be extended for their needs.

Adil, the manager of the home insurance systems, went to meet with Tim, the auto insurance manager whom he had worked with on the new Customer Information Service. He said, "Hey Tim, I heard that one of your teams recently built a service for state sales verification. We'd like to do the same, and I wanted to see if your team could extend the service to include the rules and regulations around the home insurance products. I'm sure it already has the necessary checks for sales offices."

Tim replied, "Yes, we built a service for that with our last update. Mitch was the project manager for that effort, why don't you talk to him and see what he can do."

Adil sent Mitch an email asking about the service, but wasn't happy with Mitch's response:

> *Adil, yes, I was the project manager for the last update that created that service. I've moved on to a different effort, now, however, as have the developers that worked on the project. I'm not sure whom you would even talk to about having modifications made. Sorry, I couldn't be of more help – Mitch.*

Adil went back to see Tim, "Tim, I just received an email from Mitch, and he indicated that the team that built the service has been disbanded and are all working on other things now."

"Hmm, I hadn't thought about that, but we normally do just assign resources to the next project in the queue."

"Any suggestions? I could really use this service, but I certainly can't wait until the developers are freed up to make the necessary changes."

"Is this something some of your developers could take care of?"

"Unfortunately, most of the work for this system was going to be on the front-end, so almost all of my developers assigned to it are C# programmers. Early on, the architect for the project made the assumption that we'd be able to leverage your service, so I only assigned one Java developer to the effort for some minor modifications on the back-end. I'm guessing your service is written in Java, right?"

"Yes, it was written in Java", Tim replied.

Adil's team was in a bind. His Java developer was a junior developer whom he didn't think could come up to speed on someone else's service quick enough, and Tim didn't have anyone available to make the necessary modifications. Both managers wanted to do the right thing. They contacted Elena for direction. After meeting with Elena, and going over the priorities associated with Adil's project and the auto insurance project that the original service developers were now involved with, the decision was made to delay the auto insurance project to free up the developers necessary to make the modifications to the service. Both efforts wound up being delivered far later than the original target dates for the system.

The SOA Center of Excellence

Elena called her team together to discuss the situation. "We all know that Andrea encouraged IT to adopt SOA in her Town Hall meeting last spring. Since that time, we've had two efforts that had significant delivery delays that were directly attributable to their attempts to adopt SOA. One effort had three different projects that all needed a common service, but no one wanted to step up and write it. They spent all their time arguing, and almost wound up with three separate implementations of the same thing until I stepped in to get them on the same page. Another effort from the financial services area wound up writing another Customer Information Service, when the existing one from Spencer's team could have met at least 90% of their requirements. Finally, on the last effort, the manager tried to do the right thing in reusing an existing service, but there were no developers left from the original service development project to make the necessary modifications. I don't know about you, but if I were Andrea, I'm not going to be too happy about our SOA results for the year."

One of the architects, Greg, was sitting in his chair with a frown on his face. "Elena, I know that SOA is important to Andrea, but I don't see how we could have done anything differently on any of these efforts. At least the teams were all trying to write services, isn't that a good thing?"

Spencer responded, "Greg, while I do think it's good that these projects are trying to write services, we're going to have a big problem if we keep seeing delays or redundant services. Also, keep in mind that these are only the projects that we've heard about. Who knows how many other projects are having similar problems?"

Elena said, "I agree. So, what are we going to do about it?"

Spencer replied, "While I don't want to just use the easy target that we always hear about in IT, it's definitely true that if our communication was better we could have easily avoided having the financial services team write a separate Customer Information Service. They simply didn't know about the services that already existed. If someone had made sure they knew, they probably would have used it."

Greg replied, "That's true for that situation, but what about the other two? Those teams were communicating with each other and they still ran into problems."

Spencer thought about this one, because Greg had a good point. The teams involved with these projects were talking to each other, but they all still had problems. Then it hit him. "You're right Greg, they were communicating. What they didn't have, however, was service ownership. All of the projects involved were concerned with their own needs. Those needs were not writing a service that could be used by others. Those needs were the typical needs of all of our projects, which is writing the consumers of those services, usually the user facing systems that the end users see. In the case of the address validation service, Elena had to force one of the teams to take ownership of the service and deliver it to the other teams. With the state sales verification service, Adil and Tim agreed on who owned the service, but the organization didn't back it up with any staff. Even on my own efforts back with the Customer Information Service, our initial focus was so much on what we had to do, and not on delivering the service to the consumers."

Elena stepped in and said, "Spencer, that's a very good analysis of the problem and I think I have an idea. You're absolutely right that service ownership is a new concept. So is looking for services that have already been developed when architecting a new project. This is a fundamental change in the way we do development. Change like this is never easy. Everything I've read about change recommends starting small, getting some experience under your belt, and then leveraging that experience in other areas. In order to do this, I think we need to establish a Center of Excellence for SOA."

Over the next two weeks, Elena met with several managers that had been involved with projects that were embracing SOA, and put together a team of eight people, including Spencer. The team was a mixture of architects, technical leaders, and lead analysts. Elena and three key senior managers were the sponsors of the team.

"I want to thank you all for agreeing to take on this added responsibility. Your respective managers all thought that you have a good handle on the concepts around SOA. That's very important, because your job as a team is to make sure our SOA efforts stay on track."

Jared, one of the lead analysts from the brokerage services group, asked, "I'm more than happy to help out with this effort, but I have a simple question. What do we want to do with SOA? While I understand that Andrea has encouraged us to adopt SOA, there really isn't any consensus within my area on what exactly we should be doing. Some teams think that unless something is clearly going to be reused, they don't need to do anything. Other teams think that if you're not coming out of a project with at least 10 services, you're not doing a good job."

Raj, one of the technical leaders agreed, "I've seen the same thing in my area. It ranges from some teams that are completely ignoring SOA because they don't think it applies to them, to teams that are trying to take all of their current integration points and expose them using SOAP and HTTP."

"Well, it sounds like the first task for this group is to provide some definition around what SOA means at Advasco and start getting the message out," said Elena. "At the same time, remember that we still have projects going on every single day and they're not going to stop while this team takes the time to define SOA. So, in addition to defining SOA, all of you need to be the ambassadors for your areas. You need to be aware of the SOA efforts that are occurring within your areas, and you need to share those efforts with this team. If you become aware of service development from another area that is applicable to your own area, start the conversation and get the right people talking to each other. If you find out that a team in your area is not taking the appropriate steps with SOA, whether it is reusing existing services or taking the time to find out which other teams may be able to leverage their services, you have full authority to stop that project and get them on the right track. I've spoken to all of the development managers in all of your areas, and they're all on board with this effort."

"What about the problems we've had with service ownership?" asked Spencer. "I don't feel comfortable telling these teams which one of them should be writing the service. Based upon the few examples we've had so far, sometimes there isn't a clear answer."

"Good question Spencer. I don't expect this group to make ownership decisions. Some of those decisions may challenge our current organizational structures. It is best that we allow the managers in those organizations to make those decisions. That being said, it is the responsibility of this group to escalate these situations immediately so that we can get the managers involved before it becomes a problem. So, does anyone else have any questions? If not, let's go to work and start getting the SOA efforts on track."

In line with Elena's direction, the first thing the Center of Excellence team did was to focus on defining what SOA was for Advasco, and figuring out how to communicate that message to the rest of the organization. They put together a series of presentations that explained the basic concepts of SOA and the goals that they hoped to achieve through adoption. These presentations were open to the entire IT organization, and did a great job in getting everyone on the same page.

While these initial communication efforts established their credibility, the team still had some challenges ahead of them. During the time they were putting together the presentations, their meetings were very productive. Now, however, as that work was winding down, the team was finding it hard to get involved with the projects that were going on in the organization. When the team had approached projects, the projects weren't dismissive, but they also didn't freely share information either. Most of the project teams just told the COE that they'd contact them if they needed them.

At the next meeting, Spencer brought this dilemma up. "I know we've all been struggling with figuring out how to work with the project teams. I've given it some thought, and I think part of our problem is that while we shared the reasons for why we're adopting SOA, we didn't share the reasons why this COE exists and how we expect projects to work with us."

Raj said, "I think you're right, Spencer. I can't tell you how many meetings that I've tried to set up that have either been declined or gone through an endless sequence of cancellation after cancellation."

Jared echoed the same sentiment, "I've had the same problems with project teams in my area. While I know Elena told us that we have the authority to stop projects, I simply haven't been able to get enough information out of them to even know whether I need to stop them or not."

Spencer said, "Let's go back to the original direction Elena gave us. Besides the initial communication, she indicated that we need to make sure that existing services are being leveraged where appropriate, that service ownership is assigned to the right group, and that when a service is identified, we take the time to determine what other consumers may exist. If that's what we need to do, how do we go about doing that?"

Raj replied, "Most of those questions can be answered at the early stages of the project. Perhaps we should set up a review process after the project has come up with its proposed architecture? That should be early enough that no development has started."

Spencer said, "I think that's a great idea Raj. Let's try to put that in place, but let's make sure that the projects know exactly why we're meeting with them. We need to make the review process as painless as possible."

The team went on to determine the details of the review process, as well as other things that they'd need to cover over the course of the project. The outcome was a very clear engagement model of how they would interact with the project teams. They went through it with the managers in their respective organizations, and from that point on, their level of involvement with the project efforts improved steadily.

Enterprise SOA Governance

In this chapter, Spencer and Elena find out that initial success doesn't immediately translate into continued success. It began with the CIO, Andrea, giving her personal endorsement to SOA and encouraging all of IT to embrace it. With the endorsement of the CIO, how could the effort possibly go wrong? Clearly, it didn't take much.

If we go back to our original definition of governance, it is the people, policies, and processes that an organization leverages to achieve a desired behavior. Therefore, SOA governance is about achieving a desired behavior through SOA. A simple statement of "go forth and adopt SOA" is not enough to articulate the desired behavior, yet that's exactly what Andrea did. Without more explicit guidance on what IT and the business hoped to achieve through the adoption of SOA, the results will likely be little more than just a bunch of services. The normal behavior of project teams is to only look within their own projects, so without explicit instructions to do otherwise, those project teams will continue to do so. As a result, there is significant risk of having multiple projects build the exact same service, as with the portfolio management system. Even where the projects are broader in scope and more opportunities exist, there is just as much of a chance of controversy, as with Maria, Jim and Beth, as there is of actually achieving some success with SOA.

In order to achieve enterprise goals with your SOA adoption efforts, you need to have enterprise governance. This begins with establishing and communicating those goals as the desired behavior, and then putting the people, policies, and processes in place to make it happen.

Establishing Goals

One of the things that Jared brought up in the very first meeting of the Center of Excellence was that no one had properly articulated what the desired behavior needed to be. A good litmus test to use when trying to establish the desired behavior is to look at the phrasing of the behavior and see how many different ways it can be interpreted. For example, compare the following statements.

- We want to adopt SOA.
- We want to reduce our development costs by 10%.
- We want to increase the amount of code we reuse by 10%.

It should be very clear that the latter two statements are much more explicit about the desired behavior. As with any high-level goal, there's still some room for interpretation, but clearly, the first statement, which is the message that Andrea delivered to IT, gives very few specifics. Another litmus test that can be used is whether or not the behavior can be measured. If you can't measure it, how do you know you've achieved it? So, how would an organization measure their adoption of SOA? It could be based upon the number of services created, the number of services reused, the length of time to implement solutions, or the number of solutions produced in a given time period. While broad, vague statements like, "We want to increase our agility" certainly have meaning and can rally the troops, it is the specifics that make it happen. Using our analogy of municipal government, setting goals is very important to achieving the respect and authority necessary to provide good governance. Would you rather vote for a politician that says, "I will make your standard of living better," or one that says, "I will lower your taxes by 50% over the next two years." One is at the risk of idle words, while the other has a specific behavior in mind, and is well-positioned to create the policies to get there.

When establishing the desired behavior for your SOA efforts, you should give careful thought on how to quantify the benefits. Two popular benefits frequently mentioned in the press are reuse and agility. Of the two, reuse is the far easier one to quantify, but it is also considered somewhat of a holy grail in IT circles. Many technologies and approaches have claimed reuse as a benefit, but few, if any, have lived up to the hype surrounding them, at least at the business level. At the infrastructure level, there is no arguing that popular OO frameworks, such as .NET and Java EE, have provided significant reuse to the enterprise. Despite this, reuse is still a goal of many IT managers because there typically is an underlying assumption that significant redundancy exists in the systems today. Unfortunately, it is very unlikely that the staff have performed adequate analysis to know where the majority of the redundancy is. Therefore, if one of your goals is reuse, your governance efforts will need to address the behaviors of the project teams during the architecture and analysis phases of the project. These phases are where opportunities for reuse must be discovered.

Agility is a more difficult term to quantify. To be agile is to move quickly and easily. Therefore, if an IT department wants to be more agile, that usually means that they want to have a quicker response to the demands of the business. In other words, productivity needs to improve. That means that either projects are getting delivered faster, or a higher number of projects are being delivered in the same time period, with a proportional adjustment based upon any increase or decrease in staff. Software development efforts can be more productive through reuse, since studies have shown that it takes far less time to integrate a reusable asset than it would to build it a second time. Another path to higher productivity is through increased modularity. By designing systems in a more modular fashion, the impact of change can be reduced to a smaller set of IT systems, thereby reducing the time to implement and test the change.

As an example, here are some properly formed goals around agility and reuse:

- Increase the number of assets reused by 10% each year.
- Decrease the average time to produce a solution by 10% each year.
- Increase the number of projects delivered by 10% each year.

In contrast, here are some example goals for SOA that are not as effective:

- Adopt SOA.
- Increase the number of services in the repository.
- Increase the average number of services produced by each project by 10% each year.

Clearly, the first goal is simply too vague. The latter two goals may look good on the surface, but are actually quite problematic for one simple reason. Both of these are not focused on consumption, which is the key to reuse and productivity, but the act of service production. Simply building a bunch of services could actually be detrimental to an organization as it increases the number of moving parts for any given solution. If there is no good reason to separate two units of functionality into two independent parts with their own lifecycles, they shouldn't be separated.

Roles

Once the goals and desired behaviors have been set and articulated, it can't be successful without having people who have the responsibility for making sure those goals and behaviors are followed. Remember, a goal is not a policy. A goal is an outcome; a policy is a way of guiding someone towards that outcome. If a city wants to reduce traffic accidents on a highway (the desired outcome), a policy that guides drivers towards that outcome is to lower the speed limit. Likewise, if an enterprise wants to increase the amount of reusable assets involved in solutions, a policy that guides projects towards that outcome is that all projects must review the reusable asset library as part of their architecture and analysis efforts.

In order to have policies, we need policy makers. In the example in this chapter, this began with Enterprise Architecture, but was then delegated to a cross-functional Center of Excellence that included architects, lead technical staff, and lead analysts. The key is that these policy makers must be viewed as authorities in the organization, which is perhaps the most difficult part of the entire effort. While organization charts and mandates establish some level of authority, it does not establish trust. If someone is not trusted, they will have increased difficulty in maintaining their authority. As a result, they will be more likely to gravitate towards heavy enforcement mechanisms that can further erode trust.

In any organization, there are already roles that have some amount of implied authority. Within a project structure, the roles of the project manager and the lead architect or technical leader clearly have implied authority. Within an organizational structure, the management hierarchy has implied authority. An enterprise architecture organization frequently has either explicit or implied authority on many technical decisions and architectural direction, although this authority can vary widely from organization to organization. An organization may have several standing committees that are seen as authoritative bodies, some of which may even be called governance committees.

Enterprise Architecture

Enterprise Architecture, at a minimum, normally has oversight on the technical architecture policies that guide solution development. This can range from standard hardware platforms, operating systems, database platforms, application servers, programming languages, security technologies, networking hardware, and more. In the context of SOA, Enterprise Architecture is certainly a possibility for establishing policies for Service Communication Technologies, Service Implementation Technologies, and Service Interface Specification, as discussed in Chapter 2.

In some organizations, Enterprise Architecture may also include a business architecture discipline. While the technical architecture policies are intended to guide how an organization builds and integrates services, business architecture policies are intended to guide what services an organization builds and integrates. While technical architecture can be considered at the top of the ladder for development and implementation activities, business architecture can be considered at the top of the ladder for business analysis activities.

Information Architecture

Information architecture, as the name implies, normally has oversight over the information assets of the organization. The previous chapter articulated the role of the canonical model in ensuring a consistent representation of data across services. Canonical models are usually the responsibility of the information architecture team, and play a key role in service definition. In addition to this, the information architecture team likely plays a key role in determining information classifications, which can drive the use of encryption within services, as well as information stewards and/or owners, which is a key data point when attempting to define service ownership.

IT Management

IT management normally has oversight on the IT staff within an organization. In our example in this chapter, one of the efforts described had problems with determining service ownership. This wasn't an issue with what service was being built or what technologies that were being used to build it, but with who would build it. This is not an architectural question, but a staffing question.

The biggest challenge that IT management faces with SOA adoption is that the current organizational structure may be an inhibitor of the goals SOA wants to achieve. In many organizations, teams have been aligned along the user facing components of their systems, not along some of the back-end processing components. Even in our example, Advasco had one team for home insurance applications and another one for auto insurance applications. They each had their own techniques for customer relationship management, ordering, billing, and probably much more.

Business Management

Business management, in addition to having oversight on the business staff, normally has oversight over a very critical part of the SOA effort: funding. While an IT department has control over allocation of resources, they are still normally operating within the funding constraints that have been imposed by the business units. Even when the business is technology, there is likely a separation between technologies that are used to run the business, versus technologies that actually represent a revenue stream for the company.

Developers

Developers clearly have a major role in the implementation of SOA. While not normally considered a position of authority, they are in the position of execution. In addition, there are normally far more developers than there are architects in an organization, so a great deal of policy adherence is always left to the discretion of the individual developer. Successful involvement of representatives from the developer community in the SOA governance effort can have a big impact.

Analysts

Like their development counterparts, analysts are focused on the implementation of SOA. The developer's primary concern is how services get built; the analyst's primary concern is what services get built. In addition, it is very common for the analysts to have a much stronger connection to both IT management and business management. Once again, given their role in the implementation effort, successful involvement of them can have a big impact on the overall SOA governance effort.

Database Analysts (DBAs)

The DBA is the implementation counterpart to the information architect, just as the developers and analysts are the implementation counterpart to the enterprise architect. The DBAs have added insight into the storage and utilization of data by a variety of applications, and this knowledge can be valuable during service definition. Involvement of the DBAs in the SOA governance effort and as part of the Center of Excellence is recommended.

Center of Excellence

If organizations already have authoritative bodies like Enterprise Architecture, IT Management, and Business Management, why would they need a Center of Excellence? Remember, organizational structures only position a group for authority, they don't mandate it. Only by establishing credibility and trust will a group create authority. In general, there are two reasons that organizations will create a SOA Center of Excellence.

The first is to overcome a lack of trust in the existing organizations that are positioned as authorities. Breaking down existing barriers and establishing a cross-functional Center of Excellence can quickly form a new authoritative group. When the constituents of an organization have representation on the governing body, they are more likely to trust that their interests are being represented, although it is very dependent on the representative chosen.

The second reason that an enterprise may create a SOA Center of Excellence is for focus. All three groups mentioned earlier have other responsibilities outside of SOA. As a result, SOA may not always be the top priority of their actions. By creating a Center of Excellence, these organizations can delegate responsibilities (along with other organizations that may not normally be involved with authoritative roles) to a team whose first priority is SOA. This is a very important point, because one reason many SOA efforts fail, as well as governance efforts, whether SOA or not, is that no one has it as their top priority.

Not all organizations will need a Center of Excellence. Advasco did. Your company may need it. Your competitor may not. Just as there are many styles of government in the world that can be considered successful, there are many styles of SOA governance that can be applied in an organization and achieve success with SOA. In determining whether you need it or not, look at your existing organization and how other governance in other areas is applied. If your current governance efforts are successful, you may be able to fold in policies around SOA adoption. If your current governance efforts are struggling, or the teams involved are stretched thin, a Center of Excellence may be a good fit for you. Remember that the goal of the governance efforts is to ensure that the desired behavior is achieved. The organization must always be measuring their performance against that behavior, and if the organization is not achieving that behavior, a change needs to be made.

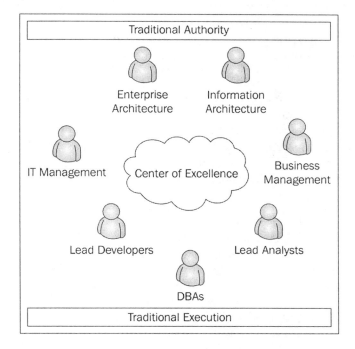

Engagement Model

Regardless of whether you choose to leverage existing groups within your organization or form a Center of Excellence, a key to success is having a well-defined engagement model. In our example, the Center of Excellence initially focused on communication to the IT organization about the goals of the SOA effort, but once that communication was complete, they struggled to remain relevant.

Any governance organization has this risk. In the context of traditional government, a frequent complaint is that the government is out of touch with its constituents. The same holds true within the IT department. Many people working in the trenches will make comments about Enterprise Architecture sitting in an ivory tower or upper management sitting in their corner offices. This implies that these workers feel that the people responsible for governance are out of touch with the work that is occurring.

In order to mediate this risk, the people responsible for governance must have a clearly defined and communicated engagement model for how they work with the projects that are occurring in the enterprise. For example, if the Enterprise Architecture team chooses to have all projects go through an architectural review in front of the entire Enterprise Architecture team, it must ensure that projects clearly understand when this review must be performed, what people need to be involved, what needs to be presented, and what the possible outcomes of the review are.

If you are leveraging a Center of Excellence, then you must decide what role it will have on projects. Will the staff act solely as a review board for projects or will individuals from the Center of Excellence be assigned to projects? If assigned to projects, will they act as mentors, or will they be actual project participants? Or, will the Center of Excellence take a different approach and act in an outsourcing capacity, with projects handing off their service development efforts to it?

There is no standard engagement model that all organizations should use. The only wrong engagement model is to not have one specified. If your organization lacks the necessary skills to build services to begin with, then perhaps an outsourcing model is the right approach, gradually increasing the size of the team to increase skills, until a critical mass is reached. At that point, the team can now be distributed back throughout the organization. However, this approach has its risks. A centralized group may have the technical skills necessary to build services, but they probably will not have the knowledge of all possible business domains where services will be built. An alternative approach to this is to be a staffing solution for projects, rather than an outsourcing solution. Rather than projects sending work to the Center of Excellence, the Center of Excellence sends resources to the projects. These resources can act as a mentor to others on the project team, or be a full-fledged member of the project, performing analysis or development activities as appropriate. By working with the project team in any capacity, the resource or resources assigned can spread the knowledge of SOA to other members of the project team.

If the organization is not lacking skills in service development, then it is more likely that the Center of Excellence exists to facilitate inter-project and inter-organization communication. This is also a scenario where an existing team, such as Enterprise Architecture may also be suitable. Regardless of whether it is a Center of Excellence or some other group, the problem at hand is that an engagement with the project team is not required for the project team to complete their work. However, it may be required in order for the project team to complete their work in a way that meets the goals of the SOA effort. In this scenario, the governance team must look at the natural checkpoints in the project effort and decide if they are appropriate for whatever reviews might be necessary.

Finally, it should be mentioned that the engagement model could be focused outside of project efforts. Rather than focusing on reviews within the project lifecycle, an organization can instead focus on education of the staff. The risk with this approach is still the project-driven culture of most organizations. If the project staff can be trusted to know when to go beyond the boundaries of the project to reach out to other teams, adjusting their own priorities and scope as necessary, it is possible to get by with only an education-based approach. Unfortunately, this level of trust, along with the necessary clarity of goals and relative priorities rarely exists within organizations. In the end, the most common approach taken by most organizations is a combination of education, mentoring, staff augmentation, and formal reviews.

Design-Time Checkpoints

Clearly, checkpoints play a key role in governance. In the previous chapter, we discussed some of the items that must be factored into the existing project governance structure. These were a natural extension of the technical reviews that normally take place in a review, factoring in technical items that are specific to service development. However, these aren't the only changes required to the project governance process.

In our example, the Center of Excellence chose an engagement model that required them to conduct reviews of the projects. In their kickoff meeting, Elena specifically mentioned that the Center of Excellence needed to:

- Share the efforts of their respective areas with the rest of the Center of Excellence
- Enable interactions between service providers and service consumers across the organization where they normally would not exist
- Ensure that existing services get reused
- Ensure that projects that are building services seek out consumers
- Escalate service ownership decisions to management

The items that were covered in the previous chapter ensure that services are built consistently. The items above, in contrast, deal more with ensuring that the project teams look outside of their project boundaries for either services that can be leveraged, or consumers that may be interested in services that the project is building.

Whether you're trying to define your review process or trying to enable the project team to make good decisions on their own, it is important to look at the entire software development lifecycle and determine the appropriate time to ask these questions. While most development projects today follow an iterative methodology, it still holds true that there are analysis artifacts, architecture artifacts, design artifacts, and development artifacts that will be produced by the project team. As each of these artifacts are produced and refined, questions can be asked within the project team or by the review team.

Analysis Checkpoint

The objective of analysis is primarily to establish detailed requirements for the desired solution. If the project or program is very large in scope, the team should also have an understanding of the business domains involved in the solution, and should be forming an idea of the business services involved and their potential consumers.

In the context of SOA, the key question that must be asked is whether or not the analysis artifacts provide sufficient detail to determine an initial set of services that are required for the solution. If the project architect cannot review the artifacts and establish a proposed architecture for the solution, then the analysis has not gone into sufficient depth.

Architecture Checkpoint

The objective of the architecture phase is to establish the major components that will define the solution. A major component is one that allows the work to be broken down into units that can be independently managed. Not surprisingly, the lines on which those components are separated normally represent candidates for service consumer and service provider relationships. It is at this point where service ownership decisions should be finalized, because the best scenario for development is to have the eventual owner involved, rather than having to do a handoff from the development team to the actual service owner. Based on this, the following questions associated with SOA adoption should be asked at the architectural checkpoint:

- Do the boundaries defined by the architecture clearly define the service consumers and service providers that constitute the solution?
- Which of the services are new, and which ones represent existing services?
- Which of the services are provided by the third-party systems or external providers?
- Have all the new services clearly identified owners, and have they been engaged?

- Have the service managers for existing services been engaged to determine if any changes are required to meet the requirements of the new consumers?

- Have all potential consumers of the new services been identified and engaged?

- Have service development efforts been sufficiently disconnected from service consumer development efforts, such as spinning them off as separate projects?

- Have all proposed services and associated business and technical metadata been entered into the service repository and/or other metadata management systems (for example, configuration management database)?

- Have all service consumers been entered into the service repository and/or other metadata management systems (for example, configuration management database)?

Design Checkpoint

The design phase of a project goes within the black boxes and focuses on implementation of the services and associated service consumers. It should be noted that what was a single program or project may now be multiple efforts. It is at this point where iterative development should begin. If the iterative process has begun too early, it is possible that the architectural boundaries may get established too late in the process, potentially after some service development has already begun. This puts the project at risk for choosing incorrect service platforms, not having service owners engaged from the beginning, and not having a complete view of all of the possible consumers for each service.

At this phase in the project, the following questions associated with SOA adoption can be asked:

- Are the service interfaces using message formats from the canonical model?

- Have initial service contracts been defined between all known service consumers?

- Has the project established service contracts with services being provided by other teams, third-party packages, or external providers?

- Do the service contracts include release schedules for milestone builds that are synchronized with the schedule for service consumer development?

- Have service types been identified for all services, and appropriate service implementation platforms chosen based on those types?

- Have the non-functional requirements of the service been appropriately externalized from the business logic of the service?

- Have all naming conventions for services (for example, URLs, XML namespaces) been followed, both for the production environment and the development environments?
- Is there an appropriate separation between the service interface (XML Schema and/or WSDL definition) and the planned service implementation?
- For Web Services, is the service compliant with the WS-I Basic Profile 1.1?
- Do all service interfaces and/or contracts address exceptions and errors appropriately?
- Are all schemas in web services externally referenced via import?
- Are attributes and child elements used appropriately within XML schemas?
- Have data sensitivity requirements been identified for all data elements involved with message interactions?
- Have transactional requirements been identified for all service operations?
- Have test cases been established for all service operations?
- Are all services free of references to implement specific details?

Implementation Checkpoints

At this point, the focus should be on how well the service implementation has adhered to the original design. While existing governance processes may focus on coding standards that apply to any development effort, there are still some additional questions that can be asked that are relevant to SOA adoption. They are:

- Have service consumers been packaged separately from service providers?
- Is the service interface appropriately separated from the service implementation, including any processing that binds or maps an internal processing model (for example, object model) to the messaging model (for example, XML Schema) associated with the service interface?

Operational Readiness Checkpoint

Prior to going live, all components of the solution should be reviewed for their operational readiness. Again, this should already be part of your standard governance practices, but when now deploying service consumers and service providers, the following questions are relevant to SOA adoption and should be considered:

- Do all services have an assigned service owner?
- Do all service consumers have an assigned point of contact?

- Have operational reports been defined for all service consumers and service providers?
- Have all records in the service repository and other metadata repositories (for example, configuration management database) been updated for the service consumers and service providers?
- Have all service contracts been finalized?

Service Portfolio Management

A consistent theme throughout this chapter has been raising the awareness of project teams to other services and consumers in the enterprise. While there's a certain amount of improvement that can happen simply through word of mouth, in general, that approach is not sustainable. For example, in the past, there were efforts to raise awareness of applications and their database dependencies. One or two select people may have had knowledge of 80% of the applications associated with one database based upon their experiences, when we expand this out to all applications and all databases the problem quickly becomes unmanageable, with no single person having the complete view. As a result, many organizations are now undertaking application portfolio management efforts simply to get their arms around the problem.

In contrast, we are in the early stages of SOA adoption and can prevent the same situation from occurring in the context of services. To do this, an organization should practice service portfolio management. The portfolio is always changing, with new services and their consumers being generated, while older services or consumers may be decommissioned. While it is certainly possible that a small organization can manage this effectively through the use of nothing more than an Excel spreadsheet, larger organizations can optimize their efforts through the use of a Service Registry/Repository.

The Service Registry/Repository

The Service Registry/Repository is one of two tools most frequently associated with SOA governance. Keep in mind that governance, first and foremost, is about people, policies, and processes. You cannot buy governance. You can, however, buy tools that can make your governance efforts more efficient, and the Service Registry/Repository definitely falls into that area.

Most companies that are adopting SOA include reuse as part of their desired behaviors. In order to be reused, consumers of those services must be aware of their existence. If they don't know that a service is available, they're going to build or buy their own, creating redundant solutions. While the processes that have been described in this chapter are intended to raise awareness of what services exist, individual members of the governance teams, whether a Center of Excellence or existing organizations, cannot be expected to know about every single service that exists, especially as the portfolio of services grows over time. Imagine going to a library where there is no card catalog (or these days, a computer-based directory), only librarians. While the librarians will probably have a better knowledge of the books in the library in comparison to anyone else, any individual librarian will only be aware of a fraction of the books available. Now, while the typical enterprise won't have as many services as a library has books, the amount of tribal knowledge is rampant. Most project documentation is exactly that *project documentation*. When the project ends, the value of the documentation does as well. The only information that is retained is what is in the minds of the project staff.

With SOA, the opportunity now exists to do this right from the beginning, and that starts with creating and preserving information about the service as early as possible. Recall that at the analysis checkpoint, the project team should be forming an idea of the services needed for the solution, and at the architectural checkpoint, the project team should have a clear idea of the services necessary. Additionally, the project team should know which of those services already exist. They can identify so by querying the registry/repository. At the same time, all of the services that aren't in the registry/repository need to be entered. The time to enter new services is when they are first identified. The reason for this is that there are always multiple projects occurring simultaneously. This creates a risk that there are two (or more) projects that will need the same service. If projects wait to enter a service in the registry/repository until it has been built and deployed into production, another project may be well into their own implementation of the exact same service before there's ever any record of its existence.

Initially, it may seem that the only role for the registry/repository in the space of design-time governance is as a human facing catalog to allow project teams to identify services that already exist, and publish the services that they create. However, it does go beyond this. First, awareness is only part of the equation. As shown in the example in this chapter, if there is no one responsible for the service after it goes into production, not just for making sure it continues to run properly, but to manage the interest that other consumers may have, the organization will have problems. The registry/repository plays a key role in managing the aspects of the consumer/provider relationship, from allowing a consumer to find the proper person to talk to, to allowing a provider to notify all consumers of a service of upcoming changes.

Additionally, there are always advances being made in the tools that are being used in the development process. At present, one of the increasingly popular tools is business process management systems. While there are many capabilities associated with these systems, one capability that they do have is the ability to build automated processes, which normally consist of an orchestrated sequence of services. They do this through the use of a graphical editor. This model-driven approach can be much more efficient for certain types of development. In order to make it even more efficient, however, a connection between a registry/repository of services is necessary so that services that need to be orchestrated in an automated process can simply be dragged and dropped into the tool. To understand the importance of the registry/repository for future development efforts, one only needs to look at two of the largest companies in the software development space. SAP, with their highly integrated suite of applications, has a registry/repository at its heart. Microsoft, as part of their Oslo strategy announced in 2007, also has a registry/repository at its heart. The need goes beyond a simple catalog, and if used properly a registry/repository can make both your governance efforts and your development efforts more efficient.

Summary

In this chapter, the examples demonstrated how a lack of clearly defined goals can impact the SOA effort. We also saw the challenges that SOA introduces into an organization that is quite used to self-contained projects without outside dependencies. They ranged from redundant services because of lack of awareness, to controversy over whose project would be responsible for a shared service, and finally to a lack of resources available to make updates to the service because the original project that built it had been completed, with the team reallocated to other efforts.

In an effort to change the behavior within projects, Advasco formed a Center of Excellence. The first task they took on was to provide definition to the SOA effort and establish concrete goals. Second, they embarked on an education effort to ensure that the development staff was aware of the desired behavior and the new policies associated with SOA. When they failed to see significant progress, the team formalized an engagement model to ensure that the communication lines between the projects and the Center of Excellence would stay open and that appropriate behavior could be monitored and enforced, if necessary.

Several important lessons were illustrated in this chapter. First, an organization must define the desired behavior and goals of their SOA efforts. An organization must be able to articulate why they are adopting SOA, and clearly state the desired outcome in a way that can be measured. If the outcome cannot be measured, then there is no way for the organization to know when their adoption efforts have been successful.

Next, once the desired behavior and goals are known, the organization must put people in place to establish the policies and processes that will ensure that the desired behavior is reached. These people can be existing teams in the organization, or it can be a newly formed team, such as a Center of Excellence. If the organization has not established the desired behavior and goals clearly, the first task of the governance team is to establish them.

Next, the governance team must define the policies that will guide the organization towards the desired outcome. For example, if the desired outcome is a 20% reduction in the time it takes to complete a typical project, the team must determine what change in the software development process will result in that 20% reduction. As a way of getting started, the team can look at the natural checkpoints associated with a typical project, including an analysis checkpoint, an architecture checkpoint, a design checkpoint, an implementation checkpoint, and an operational readiness checkpoint. At each of these checkpoints, the team must determine the questions that should be asked to determine if a project is on the right path, and then what policies need to be implemented to ensure that projects find that path and stay on it.

Finally, we explored the process component of design time governance. Governance processes do not necessarily equate with big checkpoint reviews in front of a review board. In fact, they need not be associated with enforcement at all. Governance processes can and should involve both educational processes and enforcement processes. If a team focuses too much on education, they risk putting themselves outside of the loop on project activities, putting compliance at risk. If a team focuses too much on enforcement, they risk creating resentment in the organization, since the teams will be unaware of the policies that must be followed but will still be held accountable when they fail to comply with those policies.

In creating these processes, tools can be leveraged to make the overall governance effort more efficient. While you cannot buy governance, you can buy tools that can make your efforts much easier. A key tool in the SOA governance space is the Service Registry/Repository. This tool provides the mechanism by which consumers can find out what services exist, and what team is responsible for them. This tool can also be integrated into the development environment to facilitate the inclusion of services in the new breed of graphical, model-driven platforms.

4

Service Versioning

Advasco had initial success with their Customer Information Service and then opened the flood gates for development by the rest of the organization. These efforts were successfully reigned in by the newly formed SOA Center of Excellence. Now, the team at Advasco faces a new challenge: modifying an existing service to handle the needs of a new consumer. This chapter will go over the challenges faced by the team and then present guidance for handling this situation within your own organization.

Making a Change

For the next few months, the Center of Excellence paid off. Projects were identifying services early in the lifecycle. Those same projects were successfully identifying other potential consumers of these new services. Implementation technologies were being chosen correctly and interface design was being properly done. Most importantly, everyone felt the SOA effort was on track.

By this time, it had been almost two years since Spencer's team developed the Customer Information Service for the auto insurance and home insurance divisions. While these two groups were very happy with the results, no additional teams had leveraged it. Outside of the annuity project, this wasn't a case of projects going in another direction; it was more due to lack of opportunities. That was about to change.

Spencer was eating lunch in the cafeteria when Ramesh walked up. "Mind if I join you, Spencer?"

"Hey Ramesh, it's been quite some time. Go ahead and pull up a chair."

"Do you remember two years ago you tried to convince Ryan to use your Customer Information Service?"

"I sure do. I didn't want to show my face in the annuity area for about a month after that. He really wasn't very receptive to the idea."

"Well, I have some good news and some better news for you. The good news is that about six months later, Ryan decided to leave Advasco. The better news is that we've now got a major initiative to revamp a number of our systems in the annuity department. I'd like to take advantage of the Customer Information Service as part of that effort."

"That's good news Ramesh. I didn't harbor any resentment towards Ryan, but I'm certainly happy about having another potential consumer for the Customer Information Service. I'll put you in touch with the service manager for it."

"Thanks Spencer. That would be great. We're just getting started on our architecture, so the timing is perfect."

"Let me know if you run into any problems. I'm still part of the SOA Center of Excellence, so it's still my job to make sure it goes well!"

Spencer put Ramesh in contact with the service manager for the Customer Information Service, Maria. Maria had recently transferred over after her work on the account maintenance effort, and now had responsibilities for the Customer Information Service. In the meeting with Ramesh, she brought her technical lead, Craig, with her.

"Spencer told me that you're interested in utilizing the Customer Information Service in some of the new systems you're building in the annuity department, Ramesh."

"That's right. We're rewriting a number of our systems, and based on what I remembered from Spencer two years ago, I thought we might be able to leverage the service."

"Great, I'd be happy to help you out. This is Craig, the technical lead who covers the Customer Information Service. He's here if you've got any technical questions. Have you had a chance to review the information available in the service repository?"

"I have. I reviewed the service interface, and while it certainly looks like there's enough there to warrant using the service rather than building our own, there's also a number of additional things that we'll need."

Craig responded, "What kind of changes are you looking for? Are there new operations that you need that are specific to the annuity area?"

Ramesh said, "There are two or three operations that we'd like to see, but most of the changes are actually in the message schemas for the existing operations. There are some additional attributes that we need, and some of the relationships between the attributes are different in our representation."

For the rest of the meeting, Ramesh and Craig went through the changes that Ramesh wanted to be made to accommodate his needs. In the end, it was clear that some changes to the existing schemas would have to be made. Maria asked, "We're going to need to go back and look over these changes, along with the integration approach for your existing database. What does the schedule for your efforts currently look like?"

Ramesh replied, "We're still in the initial stages of planning, which is why I wanted to make sure I talked to you now. Right now, the project sponsors would like to have something within six months, but they also know that nine months is far more likely. Since I have some flexibility in my schedule, why don't you take a week to look into the effort required for the changes, and let's work out the schedule then. Does that work for you?"

"That works for me. We'll get back to you next week with what we think it will take to implement the changes."

On the way back to their desks, Craig commented to Maria, "You know, while I don't have any concerns about getting the work done for Ramesh, I do have some concerns on how these changes are going to impact our existing consumers. Some of these changes are going to break the existing interfaces."

Maria said, "That is a concern. I know that there aren't any resources available to do any work on the home insurance side of things. Any suggestions on how we should handle this?"

Craig said, "Well, we definitely should make the existing consumers aware that a change is going to be made and at least get a clear idea of what the impact will be. If you can take care of that, I can take this to Spencer and the SOA Center of Excellence, and see what suggestions they have."

"That sounds like a good plan to me," replied Maria.

Over the next week, the Customer Information Service team did the analysis required to estimate how long the changes would take to implement. Maria used the communication features of the service registry/repository to push out a message to the existing consumers about the pending change, and as she suspected, the biggest problem was going to be the home insurance system. Due to other priorities, the earliest they could even begin to make changes to their consumer would be nine months from now, potentially three months after the service needed to go live.

Craig met with Spencer and explained the problem to him. Spencer agreed to facilitate a decision-making session to explore the different options. Representatives from all of the existing consumers were there, along with Ramesh, Craig, and Maria.

Spencer started the meeting, "I'm sure all of you saw the notification from Maria last week that some changes are necessary to the Customer Information Service in order to support its usage by the annuity department. The problem that we face is that these changes will break the existing consumers of the service, and not all of you can make the changes to your systems in the currently proposed timeframe. Let's start out by listing all possible options, regardless of whether we all presently agree or disagree on their viability."

Craig started out, "Well, if we're listing all possible options, the first one is to update the service, and then get whatever push we need from management to get resources allocated to the consuming systems so they can make the changes in the time required."

Maria replied, "Come on Craig, you know that we can't just pull resources off projects that easily."

Jason, from the auto insurance department, added, "Aren't all of these changes a result of the annuity department? Why can't they just include modifying our applications within their project scope? They already have resources allocated to their project."

Paul, from the home insurance department, replied, "Do you really want some developers that have never seen your application before mucking around in your code? I know I don't."

Spencer said, "Let's remember, we're listing all options, regardless of whether we all know that the option won't fly. We want to make sure we've explored all of the options. I'm going to just leave this as one option, since we still wind up with the same result, regardless of where the resources come from. I'll capture the concerns about the option."

Paul, from the home insurance group, added, "Okay, here's another option. Why don't we leave the existing service in place, and simply have the annuity project write a new service that just they use. Then, none of us using the existing service would be impacted."

Craig replied, "That's true, but isn't that going against everything we're trying to do with SOA? I thought we were trying to avoid redundant implementations of the same capability."

Spencer replied, "Duly noted, Craig. Just as with the last option, let's keep it on the board, and I'll make sure that your concerns are captured. Paul, that option actually triggered another one in my mind. In addition to having Maria's team write the new service for the annuity system, why couldn't they also keep the existing version of the service available in production for the rest of you? You can then migrate as your schedules allow."

Paul and Jason both replied in tandem, "That would work for us!"

Maria jumped into the conversation, "While I'm sure it would, that sets a very dangerous precedent for my team. How many versions of the service are we going to have to maintain? While it's a little bit better when all the implementations are owned by one team, we still have multiple implementations."

Jason then asked, "Isn't there a way to make the new service backwards compatible with the messages associated with the old service? That way, Maria's team would only have one implementation, but we could each continue to use our existing interface."

Spencer replied, "That's a very good question Jason. While we all agree that the service interface needs to change to support the annuity department's requirements, I don't know that any of us have thought about whether we can easily transform messages associated with the previous version to messages that will work with the new version, and vice versa. Craig, you're the one most familiar with the new proposed schemas. Do you think we could leverage XSLT to apply transformations for backward compatibility?"

"Yes, I think it's possible. The only concern I have is what impact this will have on the service implementation. Working with XSLT within Java code isn't the easiest thing to do, and as we make future modifications, that's just going to get uglier and uglier."

Spencer said, "There's another option for that. A year ago, we put some XML appliances in place for security purposes. I know they have XSLT capabilities and they're already in the request path."

Craig replied, "Of all the options, I think that one would work out the best. I really don't like the idea of maintaining multiple versions of the service, and having to maintain all of that XSLT code within the service is only slightly better. Allowing the annuity group to write their own goes against everything we're trying to do with SOA."

Spencer said, "Well, we know where Craig stands. Are there any other options that we should look into? No? Well, what does everyone think?"

Paul was first, "We know that we're not going to find resources to make the changes in all of the consumers at the same time, so that option is out. Likewise, it doesn't make sense for Ramesh's team to write their own service given our SOA goals, so that one is out, too. As for whether Maria's team maintains two versions of the service or utilizes some transformations somewhere, it really doesn't matter to me. From my perspective, both options give me the freedom to migrate at the time that works best for me."

Jason immediately added, "I agree with everything Paul just said."

Ramesh then offered his opinion, "Well, I certainly know that I don't want to give up any of my developers to work on Jason's and Paul's systems. We need every developer we can get right now. As for writing our own service, we've already been down that path two years ago, and now we're obviously changing the system again. If we had migrated to the service earlier, it would be one less thing that we had to touch as part of these changes. As long as Maria's team delivers my service on time for my projects, it doesn't matter to me what Maria's team chooses to do on their side."

Spencer replied, "Well Maria, it looks like everyone else thinks that we need a solution that will allow all of the consumers to continue to use their existing interfaces or the new one, but the details of how that happens is completely up to you and Craig."

Maria said, "Let's not jump to conclusions yet. If I'm going to maintain multiple versions, I need some kind of guarantee that the existing consumers will eventually migrate to the new version. If my team allows continuous use of the old interface for 12 months from the time the new interface goes live, would that be an adequate time to complete whatever modifications are necessary?"

Jason and Paul thought about it and decided that this was reasonable. For the past three years, they'd averaged an update every nine months.

Maria said, "I'll make sure to remind you, early and often, that the old version and its associated interfaces are going to be decommissioned. In the meantime, I'd like to first get the new version built. I'm going to need to keep both versions around initially just to compare messages. Ramesh's team can begin using the new service, and…" As she was talking, she stopped mid-sentence.

Spencer said, "Is there a problem, Maria?"

She replied, "Well, I was just thinking, how are we going to avoid having two URL's out there? The existing consumers are using a URL that points to the XML appliances, right? We want to apply transformations to that path. What URL will Ramesh's team use? We don't want to try to apply transformations to their requests."

Spencer said, "Fortunately, I don't think we'll need to do that. We'll need to talk to the team that operates the appliances to be sure, but I'm pretty sure that the appliances can apply processing based upon incoming attributes on the message. As long as we can determine which requests came from which consumer based on the message content, we should be able to control when transformations happen, while having all the existing consumers using a single URL. We'll obviously need multiple URLs behind the intermediary, but that will be hidden from the consumers."

Maria replied, "Okay, that eases some of my fears. Just make sure you find out quickly whether the appliances can handle it or not. Until we find out, can we set up a simple routing rule so that requests from the annuity group go to the new service, while the old ones stay where they are? That way, Ramesh can use the new service as soon as it is available, and Craig and his team can start working on the transformations for backward compatibility. I'd like to wait and see how that work goes before deciding whether to leave both versions out there for 12 months or to leverage the intermediary. We've never used that functionality before, and I don't want to take a chance on impacting Ramesh's schedule in case we run into difficulty. By keeping both services available in production at first, we can eliminate any dependency between the decommissioning of the old service and Ramesh's schedule."

Craig added, "From my point of view, that shouldn't be a problem. I can treat the new version as if it were a completely new service, as long as the intermediary shields the consumers from that change. I will need to check how we can manage both versions at the source code level, though."

Maria responded, "Good points, Craig. Taking all of this into account, I think this approach poses the least risk overall."

Spencer said, "Then we're all in agreement, right? Maria's team will build a new version of the service according to the new interface, and the old interface will be available for 12 months from the time the new service is deployed. Initially, both versions will be available in production, but Maria can decommission the old service before 12 months are up, so long as the new version can be made backwards compatible via XSLT transformations. Maria will notify all consumers prior to decommissioning the old service, since regression testing will be required to ensure that backward compatibility has been maintained. She will also notify all consumers as we get closer to the 12 month cutoff when the older interface will no longer be supported."

Everyone in the meeting agreed with this approach, and the teams went off and made it happen. Craig's team investigated the best way to apply the transformations, testing them using the latest Java libraries, as well as the XML appliances that Advasco had recently installed. They found that the XML appliances performed very well, and kept the programming model of the service very clean. While the Java libraries performed satisfactorily, the resulting programming model was not as clean as the team desired. With the use of the routing rules in the appliance, they were able to remove the older version of the service from production, while still supporting the older messages for the full 12 months as promised.

The Chief Information Officer's Concern

About two months later, Elena was in her monthly meeting with Andrea. Andrea brought up the subject of service versioning. "I understand there was quite a bit of debate around how to accommodate the needs of the annuity department in the Customer Information Service."

Elena replied, "I wouldn't say that there was that much debate. Spencer facilitated a decision-making session, and I encouraged all of my team to put all of the options on the table, regardless of their viability. The real debate came down to whether or not Maria's team wanted to maintain two implementations of the service in production, or two versions of the service interface in production."

"That's actually what I wanted to talk to you about. Now that we have a number of services that have multiple consumers, changes to those services could really become a problem. Maria's example is probably just the first of many to come. While we handled this one, I don't think having a facilitated session for every service change is going to scale well."

"I agree. This is a situation that we really haven't had to deal with much in the past. When our focus was solely applications, it was always the same set of end users that wanted to see some changes made. There was never a need to deal with multiple versions."

"I'd like for you to take this to the SOA Center of Excellence and have them come up with some recommendations around service versioning. Let's get ahead of this one before it becomes a problem."

The COE Tackles Service Versioning Policies

Elena met with Spencer later on in the day and relayed the conversation she had with the CIO. At the next meeting of the Center of Excellence, Spencer brought the team up to speed on the discussion between Andrea and Elena. He went through the efforts associated with Maria's Customer Information Service, and then asked the team for their thoughts.

The first person to comment was Jared, "I'm really surprised that this got Andrea's attention. I don't think any of the services that I've worked with yet have needed to be touched since version 1.0."

Another team member, Ron, concurred, "I agree. We've only had one service in my area that's had to be modified since its initial release, and in that case, it only had one consumer that moved in lock-step."

Raj countered these statements, "I have to disagree with you. In my area, we have at least five services that will be modified in the next six months. I think Andrea and Elena are right to have us look into this."

Spencer added, "Yes, remember, they didn't ask us to tell them whether there was a need to deal with versioning or not, they asked us to come up with some policies to ensure that when versioning does occur, we have some standard guidance on how to handle it."

Raj quickly offered his opinion, "I have some thoughts on this. Services are all about consumption, right? We've all said that a service is no good unless it can be consumed, right? Well, if that's the case, shouldn't we do whatever we can to accommodate service consumption? I think we shouldn't put a limit on the number of versions of a service interface that must be supported in production. In fact, I think we should make it a requirement that a service provider supports whatever interfaces are currently needed by its consumers. While my area is the one that has a number of changes coming, those changes tend to be driven by one consumer. Most of the other consumers don't change very often, probably even less frequently than when your services might change, Jared."

Jared countered, "Raj, I have to disagree with you. Trying to maintain a potentially limitless number of service interfaces would quickly become a nightmare for the service development team."

"But are you willing to sacrifice consumers for the sake of having a smaller number of interfaces to manage?" Raj asked.

Jared replied, "Remember, I've worked in the commercial software world before joining Advasco. The company I worked for had made so many different versions of our product to meet the specifications of our customers that we got ourselves in trouble. We had to make a change to a single capability, but due to all the branches that had been made in the code, the effort took months longer than it should have. As a result, we lost customers, not because we didn't make changes when they first came along, but because we had no ability to change quickly when a number of customers required the same modifications."

Raj responded, "I can see your point, however, I don't think that means the service providers can go to the opposite extreme and expect that consumers will incorporate whatever change they decide to throw out."

Spencer decided to interrupt the debate, "You've both raised two important, yet conflicting viewpoints. On the one hand, we have the service consumers. These consumers expect to have their demands met, and if there is an alternative path that meets those demands more quickly, they'll probably take it. This leads to a desire to bend over backwards to meet the demands of any consumer, even if it means having many, many versions of the service. On the other hand, we have the service providers. In order to provide good service, the team needs to keep the number of versions it provides to a minimum. While it's all managed by one team, we're really creating the exact same problem that we have today — the same logic being implemented in multiple places, and as a result, the time required to implement a change goes up."

He continued, "It seems that the thing we need to do is to come up with a policy that balances the needs of both the consumer and the provider. We clearly can't have an unlimited number of versions, but we also can't have just one version available."

Ron replied, "In the case of my area, we sometimes don't touch an application for 18 months."

Raj added, "My department is the same. I'd say that the majority of applications are only modified once every 12 to 18 months, with a few even longer than that."

Jared commented, "We have more turnover in my area. Just about everything gets released at least once a year. The few applications that don't, usually wind up getting decommissioned in the next year."

Spencer asked, "What's a realistic timeframe for service updates? In the case of the Customer Information Service, we almost went two full years without needing an update. I also know of at least two other services that have been updated every six months."

Raj replied, "Our services follow a similar pattern. I haven't seen anything that's updated more than twice a year. Some services are updated every nine months; some are updated every 12 or 15 months. There doesn't seem to be a standard pattern."

Spencer then said, "Let's look at this from a different perspective. Since it appears that all of our systems are updated at different intervals, let's instead look at what's realistic. We know maintaining one version of the service isn't enough. If we maintained two versions of the service, the worst case would be that the consumers only had six months to make their changes, presuming a new version was released every six months. If there were 18 months between versions, they'd have 18 months. If we maintained three versions of the service, the worst case now goes out to 12 months. If version 1 was in production, and version 2 was released in March, version 3 would be released in September, and then version 4 in March of the following year. That's also assuming that consumers aren't notified until the version goes live. What is more likely to happen is that version 2 would be announced early in the process. Realistically, a system using version 1 would probably have about 14 to 16 months to make their changes. For a service that is only updated every 18 months, we're now talking about three years or more to make the necessary changes."

Raj replied, "What if the service is updated every two months, or even more frequently than that?"

Spencer answered, "While it's certainly possible that a service could be updated more frequently, do we really think that the interface would change that frequently? I'm sure if we have projects that are updated that frequently, it is probably more likely to be bug fixes or other small changes that don't cause any change to the service interface. If the actual service interface does change that frequently, I think that the service team probably hasn't done a good job in seeking out potential consumers. They are probably being reactionary, and waiting for consumers to come to them. If we take the time to seek out consumers, we should be in a better position to avoid that scenario. On top of that, how many projects get completed in two months? If there were any, I wasn't involved in any of them."

Raj replied, "Yes, that's a good point. So, it sounds like three might be our magic number. Consumers wouldn't immediately have to jump to the new release, but they'd have at least one additional release cycle to acquire funding and staff to make the necessary changes."

Ron added, "I think we can live with this, but the one thing I want to be sure of is that changes aren't done in a vacuum. Just because there's a policy of three versions doesn't mean that all changes should be discussed with all existing consumers and new prospective consumers prior to committing to a release."

Spencer said, "Good point, Ron. If we don't communicate with each other, we're leaving ourselves open to problems and dealing with 'he said/she said' scenarios."

With this caveat, everyone agreed that three supported versions was a good starting point. They all also agreed that the inconsistency in release schedules of applications could become a problem in the future. All of the members of the Center of Excellence knew of at least one application that was still in use in production, yet hadn't been modified in at least five years.

Spencer made sure he discussed this with Elena when he followed up with her the policy of three supported versions in production at one time. Elena and Spencer both agreed that having applications in use for over five years without anyone touching them was actually risky for the company, since all knowledge of the system could be lost to technology changes, personnel turnover, or other reasons. By keeping the policy at three supported versions of each service, it would encourage Advasco to review and, if necessary, refresh the systems on a more frequent basis, mitigating any risk associated with these long tenured applications.

Service Versioning Policies

In this chapter, Advasco runs into the challenge of modifying an existing service. While the initial version of a service is typically developed in lock step with one or more consumers, the hopes for synchronized schedules quickly fade away when a service has two or more consumers. As shown in the narrative, there are many different ways of addressing this challenge. What is consistent, however, is that the SOA governance effort must establish policies that are consistent with the behavior desired for the company's SOA efforts.

For at least two of the options presented in Spencer's original decision-making meeting for the Customer Information Service, attendees stated that a particular option would undermine the goals of the SOA effort. One option called for the annuity team to simply write their own version of the service that they would use. This went against the goal of having no two systems implementing the same logic. It also went against the goal of having a single owner for each service capability. Another option called for the service team to maintain an arbitrary number of service implementations. While this went along with the single ownership policy, it still ended up with multiple implementations of the same logic.

We were also presented with potentially conflicting goals. Having multiple versions of the service owned by a single team results in multiple implementations, but having a single implementation that was slow and difficult to change would go against the goals of agility for the organization. In the end, the Center of Excellence recognized that agility was the more important goal, and as long as the number of versions was kept to a small number, the associated overhead on the service team was worth it.

This example demonstrates a very important point. While an organization may initially set some very high level goals and behaviors, such as decreasing the time required to deliver new business capabilities by 10%, these goals must trickle down to finer-grained policies such as the number of services that will be maintained in production.

Explicit or Implicit Versioning

When defining service versioning policies, one thing that must be considered is whether or not consumers are required to explicitly specify the version of a service that they will use or not. For example, when using a service that is accessed via HTTP, the service invocation must specify a URL. This applies whether the service requires a SOAP envelope or if the service is using a resource model provided via REST URLs. For Advasco, a URL used internally for a service will look like this:

```
http://services.advasco.com/BooksRecords/Customer
```

In this example, there is no explicit version number associated with the URL. All we can infer is that the request is directed at the host named `services.advasco.com` for a service at the path of `/BooksRecords/Customer`. In the case of Advasco, a URL naming standard enforced at a design checkpoint requires that the first portion of the path expresses the domain of the service, in this example, `BooksRecords`, while the second portion of the path expresses the service desired within the domain, in this example, `Customer`. If there were multiple versions of this service available, the version required for the request must be determined according to the identity associated with the request. Identity is normally passed through transport headers associated with the HTTP transport, or as part of the message itself. In the case of SOAP-based services, the message can contain both header elements and the message body. The WS-Security specification defines a standard location in the SOAP header for security credentials. For example, a SOAP request for a Customer Information Service may look like this:

```
<soap:Envelope xmlns:soap="http://schemas.xmlsoap.org/soap/
envelope/" xmlns:xsi="http://www.w3.org/2001/XMLSchema-instance"
xmlns:s="http://www.w3.org/2001/XMLSchema" xmlns:tns="http://www.
advasco.com/books-records/customer/nov-2008/">
 <soap:Body>
 <tns:GetCustomer>
  <tns:customer-id>abc123</tns:customer-id>
 </tns:GetCustomer>
 </soap:Body>
</soap:Envelope>
```

In this example, the namespace element of the message is `http://schemas.advasco.com/books-records/customer/nov-2008/`. At the end of the URI for the namespace, there is a month and date that can tell the recipient of the message that the schema used in this message corresponds to the November 2008 version of the Customer schema. It is entirely possible that even the namespace of the message may not contain an explicit version identifier; however, the version of the message can be determined by looking for the inclusion, or exclusion, of specific message elements.

Another example of a SOAP request could be the following:

```
<soap:Envelope xmlns:soap="http://schemas.xmlsoap.org/soap/envelope/"
xmlns:xsi="http://www.w3.org/2001/XMLSchema-instance" xmlns:s="http://
www.w3.org/2001/XMLSchema" xmlns:tns="http://www.advasco.com/">
 <soap:Header>
 <wsse:Security xmlns:wsse="http://docs.oasis-open.org/wss/2004/01/
oasis-200401-wss-wssecurity-secext-1.0.xsd">
  <wsu:Timestamp xmlns:wsu="http://docs.oasis-open.org/wss/2004/01/
oasis-200401-wss-wssecurity-utility-1.0.xsd" wsu:Id="Timestamp-
aaddaaf5-1207-44d7-a5ab-64b6bf5f678e">
   <wsu:Created>2008-05-27T21:23:25Z</wsu:Created>
  </wsu:Timestamp>
  <wsse:UsernameToken xmlns:wsu="http://docs.oasis-open.org/
wss/2004/01/oasis-200401-wss-wssecurity-utility-1.0.xsd" wsu:
Id="SecurityToken-53f28e17-d945-4966-aef1-3ab95e680721">
   <wsse:Username>jdoe</wsse:Username>
   <wsse:Password Type="http://docs.oasis-open.org/wss/2004/01/oasis-
200401-wss-username-token-profile-1.0#PasswordDigest">2gy4KlZvottIW989
aDMD6JTL/Mk=</wsse:Password>
   <wsse:Nonce>EqJ39Y6g6V+X9XgLIwx1Wg==</wsse:Nonce>
   <wsu:Created>2008-05-27T21:23:25Z</wsu:Created>
  </wsse:UsernameToken>
 </wsse:Security>
 </soap:Header>
 <soap:Body>
 <tns:GetCustomer>
  <tns:customer-id>abc123</tns:customer-id>
 </tns:GetCustomer>
 </soap:Body>
</soap:Envelope>
```

In this example, neither the URL for the request nor the XML namespace gives any indication of the version of the service desired. The only thing this message has is the identity of the consumer. This example uses the WS-Security UsernameToken profile and specifies a username of `jdoe`. Through the use of a service contract, this consumer can now be associated with a particular version of the service via policies. An intermediary can receive the message, check the policies associated with the contract for this consumer, and then either route to the appropriate endpoint or apply transformations to preserve backward compatibility.

Extending the Service Contract

In Chapter 2, we introduced the service contract, which is an explicit representation of the relationship between a consumer and a provider. The contract initially focused on providing a functional interface, along with a delivery schedule, if the service did not exist yet. However, there is much more to the service contract. The contract needs to also specify the policies that govern the run-time behavior of the service. In the example in this chapter, two run-time policies are required to enable the behavior that was described. The first is that the request needed to contain appropriate credentials to identify the source of the request. The second is that the request needs to be routed to a specific version of the service. While this may not seem important with the initial service implementation and its consumers, as soon as the next consumer comes along and requires a modification, as was the case in our example, this policy becomes very important.

Policy-Driven Infrastructure

One reason for the formalization of the service contract is to allow the infrastructure to easily enforce the policies. First made popular in the context of web access management solutions, policy-driven infrastructure has four primary components as shown in the following figure:

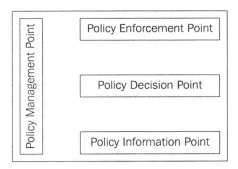

The first component is the policy management point, also known as the policy administration point. This is where the administrator would enter the policies associated with the service contract. The policy management point would also be the place where management services would be exposed for data center automation opportunities.

The second component is the policy information point. This is the backing repository where policies entered via the policy management point are stored. When applied to SOA, the Service Registry/Repository can play the role of the policy information point.

Moving into the actual run-time path of requests, the third component is the policy enforcement point. This is where requests are intercepted and any applicable policies are enforced.

The final component, which is frequently co-located with the policy enforcement point, is the policy decision point. This is where the decision is taken on what to do when enforcing each policy.

To understand the relationship between a policy enforcement point and a policy decision point, consider a real world example. If you are driving a car and reach an intersection with traffic signals, you are at the policy enforcement point. All cars must pay attention to the state of the traffic signal to determine whether they can proceed in their desired direction or not. The traffic signal itself is the policy decision point. Based upon embedded sensors in the street or timers, the light is either red, amber, or green, which represents the decision on how to handle traffic from each direction. In this example, the policy enforcement point and the policy decision point are co-located.

Now, suppose you have driven your car to the entrance of a gated community. The gate, however, is unmanned. Instead, there is either a video camera or an intercom at the gate. The gate represents the policy enforcement point. The policy decision point, however, is not at the gate. The policy decision point is wherever the security personnel is sitting watching the feed from the camera or listening to the audio from the intercom.

Putting this in the context of our versioning example, a request from a service consumer would be intercepted by the policy enforcement point. The policy enforcement point would extract the message content, and hand it off to a policy decision point. The policy decision point would examine all applicable policies for the service requested from the policy information point. There will be some policies that are universally applied, such as requiring that some form of identity be on all service requests. From that point, the identity can be authenticated and authorized, according to the policies in the service contract. Once identity is established, policies that may be specific to the service contract between the specific consumer associated with the identity provided and the service being requested can be enforced, such as what version of the service should receive the request, and whether any of the transformations will be applied. All of these policies should already be in the policy information point as a result of previous actions by an administrator via the policy management point.

Mapping this conceptual approach to the actual infrastructure associated with your SOA efforts typically takes one of the following two forms, or a combination of the two.

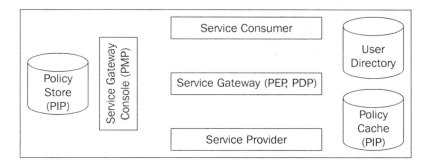

This model is a gateway-based approach (or brokered gateway pattern). A service consumer never interacts directly with a service provider; rather the request is first directed through a gateway that is responsible for policy enforcement and policy decisions. More often than not, the gateway also maintains a cache of policies locally to avoid having to establish a connection with the policy management point for every service request. The management console for the service gateway is the policy management point. This will include some form of backing stores for the policies.

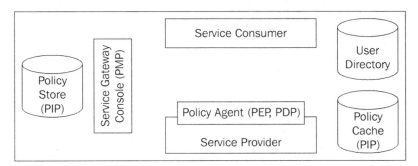

In this agent-based model, an agent is deployed on the service provider platform. This agent is typically configured as part of the platform configuration and not as part of the actual service. The agent plays the exact same role as a service gateway, with the only difference being that it performs its logic in the same execution thread as the actual service, should the policies allow the request to be processed.

While these two diagrams represent two common approaches, individual vendor products in this space can take different architectural approaches. Some may externalize the policy decision point, changing the role of the cache to be a decision cache, rather than a policy cache. Some may utilize a service registry/repository for the policy store; others may require the use of a dedicated database. Some products may include both gateways and agents, and some may even include consumer-side agents in addition to the more typical provider-side agents.

Applying Policy

In order to enforce the two policies mentioned earlier, which were:

1. All requests must contain appropriate credentials to identify the source of the request.
2. Based on the source identified, requests must be routed to the appropriate version of the service.

the basic operations would be:

1. In the policy management point, configure a policy for the service endpoint that applies to all consumers which states that only requests that contain credentials in the format desired will be allowed. Any request that does not contain credentials, or contains credentials in the wrong format will be rejected.
2. In the policy management point, for each authorized consumer, define a policy that routes the request to the appropriate endpoint or applies appropriate transformations to the incoming request and outgoing response.

The policy enforcement approach can be thought of as a pipeline of decisions, ultimately resulting in a rejection of the request or the correct routing to the appropriate endpoint. Visually depicted, it looks like this:

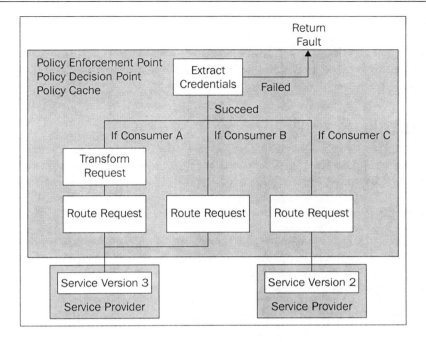

There are a number of different categories of vendor products that are capable of providing this concept of policy driven infrastructure, providing a platform for the implementation of the policy pipeline as seen in the preceding figure.

Enterprise Service Bus

Perhaps the most common of the categories, the **Enterprise Service Bus**, or **ESB**, is considered by many to be "the technology" associated with SOA adoption. In reality, an ESB is just one way of providing the capabilities associated with consumers and providers.

There is no standard architecture for an ESB. Some vendors use a gateway-based approach exclusively, others are exclusively agent-based architecture, and others provide both. The one common thing in all of them is that the ESB represents the policy enforcement point. Enterprises that have adopted ESB technologies typically require that all requests go through it, and take measures to ensure that requests which are not sent through the ESB are not allowed.

The biggest risk that an organization may face with an ESB is that many of these products are targeted at developers. As a result, the separation of policies, or even the notion of a policy itself, may not be as clear as with other solutions. This will certainly vary by vendor; therefore, an analysis of the conceptual model of the product should be part of your evaluation process.

XML Appliances

A second category of products that can provide this policy-driven infrastructure is XML appliances. These products primarily started in the XML acceleration space, expanded into perimeter security for XML over HTTP transactions, and now provide broader capabilities for additional policy domains associated with service connectivity. Some vendors are now marketing their appliances as ESBs.

Being appliances, these products typically adhere to a gateway-based model, although some of the vendors in this space create appliances by placing software on a commodity hardware platform. Those that have taken this approach may have the ability to repackage the software for installation as an agent.

The XML appliances are less likely to have a developer-centric operating model. They are more likely to present an operational model that is targeted towards an operations team rather than a development team, although just as with ESBs, there is significant variability from vendor to vendor.

Service Management Platforms

The next category of products in the space of policy-driven infrastructure is the service management platform. Unlike the typical systems management product, which normally observes system behavior in the background, products in the service management space take a more active role. In addition to collecting metrics about service invocations, they can also intercept requests and enforce policies associated with those invocations.

Service management products from the major vendors in the space will include both gateways and agents, as well as agents for other gateways, such as ESBs or XML appliances, as if this space wasn't confusing enough. A key difference between service management platforms, ESBs, and XML appliances is typically in the policy domains supported. For all of these products, the policy domains usually include ones focused on individual requests, such as security, but where the service management platforms really shine is in policies that apply across multiple requests, or policies that are consumer-based, rather than service-based. For example, service management platforms will typically be able to enforce a policy that mandates notifications whenever the average response time for a specific time period exceeds a particular threshold. Taking this concept a step further, a service management platform should also be able to apply different thresholds for different consumers. Beyond policy enforcement, service management platforms also include advanced capabilities in collecting metrics on service traffic, along with sophisticated dashboards, reports, and analytics capabilities on those metrics. In contrast, a service management platform may not have as sophisticated routing capabilities of an ESB or the raw performance or threat protection capabilities of an XML appliance.

Service Invocation and Exposure Frameworks

The final category that must be included is frameworks, specifically service invocation and exposure frameworks. As mentioned earlier, a gateway is not required to implement policy-driven infrastructure. A service invocation framework can be used to intercept outgoing requests and perform policy enforcement and decision-making, and a service exposure framework can be used to intercept incoming requests and perform policy enforcement and decision-making. For example, in the domain of security policies, a service exposure framework such as .NET and Windows Communication Foundation or Java EE and JAX-WS, allow security policies to be specified in an external file from the actual service implementation code.

Many of these frameworks have also extended the normal **WSDL (Web Services Description Language)** to specify policies for using the service, such as what type of security credentials are required. These policies are normally specified using the WS-Policy framework, but beyond security (WS-SecurityPolicy), and reliable messaging (WS-ReliableMessagingPolicy), additional standards for specifying policies have not been created. By including these policies within a WSDL document, a consumer can ensure the messages they send are compliant with what the provider expects.

The primary drawback to utilizing frameworks, and also common to an exclusively agent-based approach, is that it limits the domains of policies that can be enforced. In this chapter, the key focus was service versioning. This is an area where a framework-based approach may be insufficient. The reason is that by the time we reach the policy enforcement point, we are already executing a particular version of the service. At that point, it is too late to redirect the request to a different version, unless the versioning logic is coded into the service itself. Agents may have a bit more flexibility in this area, but if the versions aren't running in the same application server or application server cluster, there may still be challenges.

Conceptual View

While not required, it is possible to combine all of these elements into a single view. XML appliances, with their advanced security capabilities, excel at the perimeter, ESBs with their mediation and routing capabilities can act as a centralized broker, and Web Service Management agents can be leveraged throughout. Combined with the core Web Services and XML support provided by a framework yields the following conceptual view. Policy enforcement and decision points are labeled with PEP/PDP, policy information points are labeled with PIP, and policy management points are labeled with PMP.

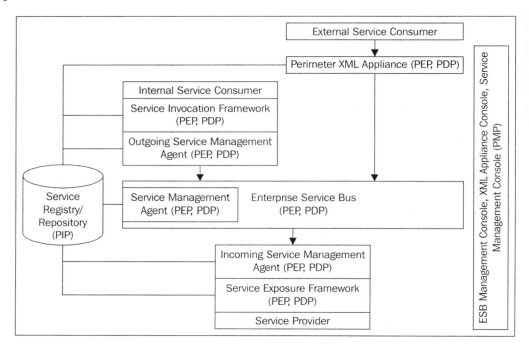

Service Lifecycle Management

The ability to enforce policies at run time is very important to SOA. In our example, the need to do this was introduced when the Center of Excellence determined that organizations managing the service must support up to three versions in production. Keeping in line with the definition of governance, the Center of Excellence recognized that the desired behavior was to support the changing needs of consumers while not overburdening the team providing the service. Remember, however, that governance is about people, policies, and process. In this case, the policy exists, but to ensure things are successful, appropriate processes must be put in place. This process is service lifecycle management.

Consider how our example could get worse, despite the policy that was put in place by the Center of Excellence. There were several assumptions that were made by the Center of Excellence in coming up with the policy, largely around the frequency of changes that would be necessary for a service, or a consumer. As an organization embraces SOA, the number of interdependencies between systems will increase. Previously, organizations may have only updated applications every 12 to 18 months, and those updates were self-contained to the application itself. Now, due to the increased number of interdependencies, those updates may involve other components outside of the application's direct control. Look across many applications, and the possibility exists that a service gets one request for a change every month for four months straight, and then a period of no changes for several months.

In order to mitigate this, an organization must change the way that these changes are managed. As a point of comparison, let's look at the interaction that organizations have with their technology vendors. When an organization runs into a bug, or requests a new feature, it normally isn't delivered on its own. Rather, the vendor maps the feature request to their release schedule, and delivers it as part of a collection of features and bug fixes that were requested by a variety of customers. If an organization doesn't adopt a similar approach for its internal development efforts, they run a risk of being crippled by the interdependencies that were intended to increase agility, not stifle it.

Service lifecycle management takes a product management approach to services. Rather than viewing service development as a project that ends when the service is placed into production, the lifecycle of a service needs to be viewed as a process of continual change and improvements, each one occurring through a managed release. This can be a difficult concept to grasp when an organization is used to thinking only in terms of projects.

The typical project, when viewed in the large sense, involves an analysis and definition phase that refines the scope of the effort, a design and development phase, a testing and debugging phase, and finally, deployment into production. The project begins when funding is approved, and ends when the solution is deployed into production and accepted by the sponsors. This effort is linear, with a clear beginning and end, as shown here.

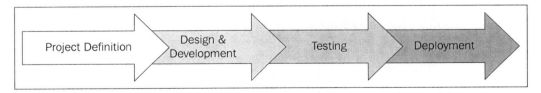

Interestingly, the project does not include any effort to monitor and manage the solution after it goes into the production. While the project may put these processes in place, if there are changes required based upon production monitoring, the project team is no longer in place to address it. A support team may exist, but these teams are normally focused on bug fixes and troubleshooting, at most. The resources that are needed to make incremental changes are more than likely assigned to new efforts.

A product management-based approach no longer views things in terms of a single linear effort with a clear beginning and end. Rather than being based on the project, the lifecycle is based on the product. The lifecycle begins when the need for version one is identified and funded, and ends when the last remaining version is decommissioned from production. In between those two events, there are any number of releases, each having the characteristics of the typical project: analysis and definition, design and development, testing, and deployment. The missing elements that tie it all together are the three M's: monitoring, management, and marketing as shown in the following figure:

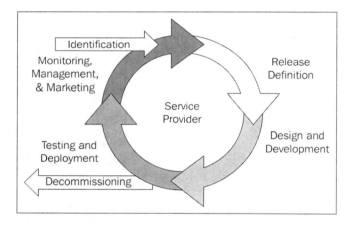

These three M's are critical to getting out of the habit of linear projects and into the world of product management.

Monitoring

The first of the three M's is monitoring. Clearly, most organizations have monitoring in place. Normally, this monitoring is focused on up/down behavior. Is the solution up and running, or is something wrong that needs to be fixed? This type of monitoring is very reactionary, and solely concerned with the behavior when something goes wrong, and not at all concerned with the behavior when things are running normally. When performing service monitoring, the focus needs to shift from the internal operations of the service to an external viewpoint on the behavior of the service. What is the response time being seen by consumers? How does the response time vary during the day? How is the response time changing over a week, a month, or several months? By observing the behavior when things are working normally, a service manager can take a very proactive approach, not only to problem detection and resolution, but also to anticipating future needs.

Management

The second M is management. Monitoring of the service is typically an activity only performed by the service provider. In order to truly be proactive, a service manager must take that information and discuss it with their service consumers. If the monitoring indicates some level of unusual behavior, be it a slow, but steady increase in response time, or anomalies in usage patterns, the service manager must discuss it with the consumers to determine the root cause. It is in these discussions that new feature requests may arise, changes being made to the existing interface in order to better support the usage patterns, or even changes being made to the consumer, based upon the observations that have been made.

Marketing

The final M is marketing. Management is focused on existing consumers. Marketing is focused on new consumers. Many organizations take a "build it and they will come" approach, and all too often find out that nobody comes. While governance certainly plays a role in trying to ensure that projects find the services that they need for their solution, service providers should not rely solely on governance for finding new consumers. A service manager must take an active role in marketing the capabilities available. Back in Chapter 2, Spencer did this, albeit unsuccessfully, for the Customer Information Service. In the end, this effort paid off because Ramesh came back to Spencer when an opportunity to leverage the service presented itself again.

As these activities continue, the service manager can now begin forming plans for the next release in a proactive manner, rather than waiting to begin the cycle until the next consumer comes along and requests it. If a service manager is successful in these efforts, they can begin to plan out scheduled releases on a regular basis. This is the key to effective version management. If consumers know that a new release will be produced and deployed every six months, they can plan their own releases around that effort. If, instead, releases occur on an ad hoc basis, it is far more difficult for an existing consumer to respond to those changes.

Summary

In this chapter, Advasco was faced with the challenge of service versioning. A new consumer had requested some changes to the Customer Information Service, but the existing consumers could not accommodate the changes necessary in the timeframe required. Led by the SOA Center of Excellence, a decision-making process was used to determine the best course of action, which was to support both the old interface and the new interface, either by deploying two versions of the service, or leveraging transformations in the middle to ensure backward compatibility.

While this solved the situation for the Customer Information Service, the CIO was concerned that this would not be the end of the versioning debate. The Center of Excellence debated this and introduced a policy that balanced the needs of the service consumers with the needs of the team providing the service. The policy was to support up to three versions of a service in production.

Service versioning is a very important issue for an enterprise to deal with in order to achieve the agility goals desired. If policies are not established, contention will arise. It can be between individual consumers of the same service, or between consumers and the service provider.

The need to support multiple versions also introduces the role of policy-driven infrastructure in a run-time environment. If multiple versions of the service are deployed simultaneously, there must be a mechanism for routing requests from specific consumers to specific versions of the service. The version desired could be explicitly specified as part of the request, or the service contract can be used to define a policy that can be implicitly enforced by the run-time infrastructure.

Policy-driven infrastructure has four key components. First, a policy management point allows policies to be administered. Second, a policy information point allows policies to be stored and retrieved. Third, a policy enforcement point exists in the run-time path of the request, intercepting it to allow policies to be enforced. Finally, a policy decision point is where decisions are made based upon the message content and the policies that are applicable to the interchange at hand.

Examples of policy-driven infrastructure include the ESB, XML appliances, service management platforms, and service frameworks.

However, policies and infrastructure alone may not allow versions to be easily managed. By changing the culture of the organization from one that deals with change on an ad hoc basis to one that anticipates change, versioning can be managed much easier.

Organizations today typically provide technology capabilities through the use of projects. A project lifecycle has a clear beginning and end, but the solutions produced by those projects do not. This creates a mismatch when a solution needs to change, because a new project with potentially new staff must be justified, funded, and completed.

An alternative to the typical project-based thinking is to embrace service lifecycle management. Service lifecycle management encourages service teams to view their service as a continual sequence of refinements, with the lifecycle rooted not in the project timeline, but the service's timeline. It begins when version 1 is approved and funded, and ends when the last remaining version of the service is decommissioned from production. The key difference in this approach is between the time a service is deployed into production and the time the next release begins, the service team must focus on monitoring, management, and marketing. Monitoring records the behavior of the system, beyond simple up/down monitoring, management utilizes the data collected by the monitors to increase the understanding of the system behavior by both the service provider and the service consumers. Marketing is focused on finding new consumers in a proactive manner, rather than relying solely on the staff of new projects to properly search the service registry and repository.

By practicing good service lifecycle management, a service team can determine the appropriate timeframe for its releases. Just as enterprises prefer when their major technology vendors provide updates on a regular basis, so should an enterprise's internal service providers schedule their updates. By providing new versions on a regular basis, there will be no surprises for the existing consumers when changes are announced.

5
Governing the Analysis Process

The previous chapters have focused on answering the question; "How do I build services the right way?" That's only a part of the SOA equation. Another equally important, if not more important, question is; "How do I build the right services?" This chapter will present what happens at Advasco when their efforts begin to stagnate due to challenges in determining the "right" services, and discuss techniques and artifacts that can be used in governance of the analysis process.

Building the Right Services

The enterprise architecture team had gathered for their regular meeting. After covering the administrative material, Elena asked Spencer for an update from the SOA Center of Excellence. Unfortunately, Spencer's news wasn't as positive as she had hoped.

"Well, to be honest, I feel like our progress has stagnated a bit. While we're still staying busy with many of our education efforts, especially around Service Lifecycle Management, it still doesn't feel like we've reached the tipping point on our projects where we're seeing a lot more composition and reuse. In fact, it seems that we have a mad scramble at the beginning of every project to make adjustments to the services that they need, get new services created, and so on. While the architects are doing all the right things in identifying the needs early, and getting the right groups involved, it still feels like we're doing everything just-in-time," said Spencer.

He continued, "Another thing that concerns me is the number of changes that have been made to some of the services. While we've been able to handle the version changes, some of the services have had pretty dramatic changes in scope from their original version."

Elena asked, "Didn't those service teams seek out other consumers when they were first developed?"

Spencer answered, "Largely, yes. Some of them didn't seek them out properly until their second version, as they were created while the Center of Excellence was just getting formed."

"That is troubling. Do me a favor and make sure you personally review the next project that encounters this same just-in-time behavior and see if you can determine what the root cause is."

It didn't take long before Spencer had his opportunity. The very next project that came along set in course the just-in-time behavior that he had just described to Elena. This project was from the Brokerage Systems division. The project architect had done his work properly in building a candidate architecture. It called for several services, some of them new, while others were existing services identified from the repository. The collection of services certainly covered the needs of the project sufficiently. One of the new services that the architect identified was a portfolio proposal service. The project team entered into discussions with the Center of Excellence to determine the appropriate owner for this service. This is where things got complicated.

Jared, a lead analyst from the Brokerage Systems division and member of the COE, reviewed the proposed architecture and felt that the portfolio proposal service shouldn't be a new service. He asked Alan, the project architect for the new system, about this. "Alan, I see that one of the services you're going to need is a portfolio proposal service. Had you considered talking with the team that currently provides the portfolio management service about this?"

Alan replied, "We did see that service in the repository, but when we looked into it, it was clear that the service focused on operations that dealt with real portfolios, not proposed portfolios."

Jared said, "Did you discuss it with Jim, the service manager for it?"

Alan responded, "Well, no, because it was pretty clear that it didn't provide anything that we currently needed."

"Well, before we rule this option out, let's get together with Jim and discuss it. At a minimum, there's a good chance that Jim's going to be involved one way or another, since I don't think the project team is the appropriate owner for this service."

Jared and Alan met later on in the week with Jim, the service manager for the portfolio management service. Jared kicked off the meeting. "Jim, we wanted to get together with you to discuss the needs of the new system on which Alan is working. Alan, can you go over the new service you identified?"

"Sure," Alan replied. "One of the services we need is a portfolio proposal service. This application is focused on the sales process. As a result, it's only dealing with prospective customers, and not any real clients. Our financial consultants will be putting together proposals for these prospects based upon whatever existing holdings they choose to disclose. We saw that you had a portfolio management service available, but it appears that it only deals with actual portfolios held by current clients."

Jim replied, "Yes, that's true. To be honest, we've never even thought about adding proposal capabilities to the service, and you're the first person to even ask about it."

Jared replied, "So what do you think? To me, it makes sense to incorporate the proposal capabilities into the existing portfolio management service. For many clients, the portfolio lifecycle begins with the proposal to a prospect, not when the prospect becomes a client and transfers their holdings. If we want to keep things aligned with the business definition of a portfolio, I think that's the way to go."

Jim said, "It's hard to argue with your logic, but just understand that incorporating in the notion of a prospect and a proposal represents a pretty big change to the way the service is currently designed. Everything is driven off the existing holdings and customer tables. As far as I know, those databases aren't capable of storing information about prospects and proposals."

Jared could see where Jim was going with this, knowing that his team would be hard-pressed to deliver this service in the timeframe needed by Alan, even without considering the impact to existing consumers. It was apparent that Alan felt the same way, as he had a look of concern on his face. Despite that, Jared said, "Jim, let's assume for a second that we treat this as a separate service. Given the domain of functionality, it's very likely that it's going to be assigned to your team anyway. We can see what we can do about providing some additional resources to your team for the effort, but ultimately, I think the decision is up to you and whether you want to manage an additional service or incorporate this capability into the existing portfolio management service. The business is really focused on growing the investment business and drawing customers away from our competitors, so I think we're going to see more and more requests for proposal capabilities with a desire to move the data easily into a live portfolio once we get their business."

Jim thought about this and agreed. "I think you're right Jared. Alan, let's schedule a detailed discussion on the capabilities you're looking for and get the ball rolling on it. However, I can't guarantee that we're going to meet your schedule needs. We have five existing customers for the portfolio management service, and they're going to need to perform regression testing on any changes that we make."

Alan said, "Well, let's have the discussions and see where we're at. I had already talked to our project manager about adding resources to handle the development of this service, so perhaps I can have them work with you and minimize the schedule impact."

Jim and Alan got together with their teams and hashed out the details of the effort. It became clear that Alan's project would necessitate extending the schedule by six weeks in order to accommodate the work associated with the portfolio service. In addition to Alan's project, two of the five existing consumers also had plans to incorporate proposal capabilities into their systems, so their requirements needed to be factored in as well.

Jared brought this news back to Spencer and the Center of Excellence at their next meeting. Spencer asked the obvious question, "How did we miss all of this back when we created the original portfolio management service? Didn't Jim's team seek out the existing consumers beyond the initial project?"

Jared replied, "Yes, he did, but as he told us, that subject never came up. My suspicion is that the conversation began with a focus on portfolio management capabilities for existing customers with existing portfolios, and directed the thinking from there. No one ever stopped to think about proposals and prospects. So, there really wasn't anything that anyone did wrong on the project, given the context that they had. The only thing I can say is that if they had a different context going in, such as additional domain knowledge of how portfolios work in the business, perhaps these opportunities would have been identified earlier."

Later that day, Spencer met with Elena and briefed her on the situation. Elena asked, "How widely has the schedule slip been communicated? I'm concerned that this is becoming a trend. I've heard at least two other projects that have encountered similar slips in their schedule, even though it seems like we're doing all the right things as far as SOA is concerned."

Spencer replied, "I'm not sure who's aware of it outside of the project manager."

Elena soon found out that many people were aware of the problem, including Andrea. In their next one-on-one meeting, Andrea asked, "Elena, are you aware of the schedule slips we've had recently?"

She replied, "Yes, Spencer had just briefed me on the latest one, a six-week slip associated with the work that's needed to modify the portfolio management service. I've had the COE look at it, and they've struggled to identify the root cause. The project teams and the service managers have all been following our directions to the letter. The only common thread is that all of the services that have required significant rework have been due to additional capabilities being added that weren't originally included or ever known."

Andrea replied, "I know you've got a great group of people on your COE, but why don't you pull in some of the leading service managers that have experienced this first hand and see what they have to say."

Elena replied, "I'll get right on it."

Two days later, Elena sat with six key service managers including Jim, manager of the Portfolio Management service, and Maria, manager of the Customer service.

Elena said to the managers, "We're here to determine why all of your services have encountered very significant changes over their lifetime. I fully expect that your services will change, but you've all had some large addition of capabilities that weren't part of the original design, despite actively seeking out new consumers."

Jim said, "You've got that right. We went from having a service focused on retrieval and updates to existing customer portfolios to having to support prospective customers and portfolio proposals for both prospects and existing consumers. This was something that no one on our team or any of our previous consumers had even discussed, and now the project that needs it has been delayed by six weeks."

Maria added, "I've had similar problems, and have been thinking about it ever since I heard about the situation from Jim. In all of our cases, it made sense for the new capabilities to be folded into our services, but there were also other things that we had never thought about. When I think about what could have changed, it would have required some project at the time to have a different scope that would have caused us to think differently. To be honest, my team first thinks about the consumer at hand, and then takes the proposed service to others, using the initial consumer as a point of comparison."

Elena replied, "I like where you're going with this Maria, please continue."

"Well, what happens when we do this is that we bias the conversation towards the capabilities we know. As a result, the project teams aren't thinking about what capabilities they need, they're thinking about the service and whether or not the functionality it offers is something they could use, rather than coming to the table with an existing need. In other words, we're constrained by the analysis efforts of the projects at hand. Nowhere do we do any kind of analysis that goes beyond the known project. When we talk with other projects, we immediately steer the conversation towards a validation of the known capabilities rather than allowing the project to identify what they might need first."

Jim added, "I think I can simplify this even more. How do we know the services we're building are the right services not just for the project and the other initial consumers, but for the enterprise? Today everything begins from the scope defined by that initial project, which puts up some artificial barriers, even when talking to consumers outside of that project."

Mark, another manager, asked, "It sounds like we need a better way of doing analysis. Can't we leverage some of the new business process analysis and modeling techniques? Everything I've read about it seems to indicate that it looks across applications, rather than within one."

Elena responded directly to Mark's suggestion, "Mark, you're right that the business process analysis is a different way of looking at things and can provide some benefit. The problem, however, is that our business process efforts are all also tied to projects. Our first experience with it showed that we merely moved the risk. Let me draw a picture for you to illustrate what I mean. If we look at where we were with our applications two or three years ago, we had a picture that looks like this:

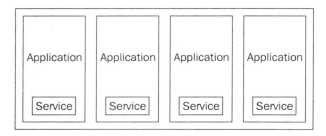

"We had vertical application silos, each that may have had some services that were very specific to them. What we've been working towards is more sharing of services across applications, a picture that looks like this:

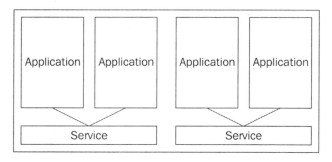

"While we've made some progress towards making these services more broadly acceptable, it seems to be happening just in time, and with more changes than we'd like when we add a new consumer. Now, let's look at this from a business process perspective. Business processes are viewed horizontally, going across applications, so we now have a picture like this:

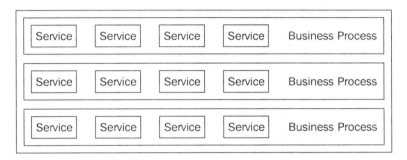

"You can see that we don't automatically get sharing of services across multiple business processes, simply by changing our perspective on things. We still have the same problem, only rather than seeking out additional applications as consumers after a service have been identified, we seek out additional business processes, so we can hopefully get to a state like this:

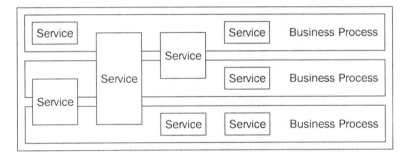

"In this state, we now have services that are shared across business processes. The point of all of this is to show that taking a business process view doesn't necessarily get us anywhere closer to the 'right' services on the first try. It merely changes our question from 'What other applications are interested in this service?' to 'What other business processes are interested in this?'"

Mark responded, "I see your point. Wouldn't having both a business process viewpoint and an application viewpoint help things out?"

Elena said, "That's possible, and certainly better than not changing anything."

Maria, who had been looking very pensive while Elena illustrated her concepts, brought forward a suggestion. "You know, it seems the common element in both of these is the constraints imposed by the project at hand. The application project influences the service definition by the constraints of the application being built, while a business process project influences according to the constraints of the process. In both cases, we get a sub-optimal service. The more I think about this, the more I think the answer to the problem lies in performing analysis outside of the context of the project."

Mark had a very quizzical expression on his face. "I'm not clear on what you're trying to say, Maria. Analysis is a core part of the project lifecycle. Are you suggesting that projects shouldn't have an analysis phase?"

Maria replied, "No, there's always going to be analysis required to do a project. What I'm thinking is that the projects need some analysis artifacts to guide them going into the project."

Elena jumped into the conversation. "This sounds very similar to what we did in technical architecture in the past, now applied to the functional analysis space. Mark, maybe this will help. Ten years ago, Advasco didn't have an enterprise architecture program. All technology decisions were made within projects, and they typically picked whatever technology was going to be best for their needs. We realized that we had several different projects that had purchased competing technologies for virtually the same problem. For example, we had at least five different Java application servers. Andrea formed the Enterprise Architecture team to help reduce our technology footprint and establish standards for technology usage. Initially, we had some success in consolidation, but we also ran into challenges when the standard platform was insufficient. When that happened, it was a mad scramble to get a solution in place. The way we solved that problem was to separate the role of the project architect from the enterprise technology architect. The project architects continued their focus on ensuring projects used technology in the ways outlined by the standards, but the enterprise technology architects operated outside of the context of any project. Their job is to continually watch what's going on in the industry, review the efforts of the project architects and their successes and failures, and with this, keep our enterprise technology architecture up to date. This architecture is the tool that project architects use to know what the 'right' thing is. Maria, if I'm getting you right, you're suggesting that what we focus on is an effort to establish a similar architecture for our functional analysis efforts."

Maria responded, "That's exactly it! I was struggling with a way to describe it, but you nailed it."

Jim was not so eager. "Elena, while I agree that this would be a good thing, I don't see a way that we can make this happen. It's hard enough to find decent analysts for the projects in the queue, how are we possibly going to pull any of them away to work on this effort? They'd have to be some of our best people to accomplish what you suggest, and those are the people that are absolutely critical to our current project efforts."

Elena replied, "I never said that this effort was going to be easy. We went through similar struggles in the early days of Enterprise Architecture. I'll take it up with Andrea and see if we can get the ball rolling. Thanks to all of you for this discussion. I think we're on the right track with a potential solution to this, we just need to make a convincing case."

The next week Elena met with Andrea to discuss the suggestion. Elena went over with Andrea the conversation that she had had with the service managers. After listening to Elena's recap, Andrea related that she had similar trepidations to Jim. "Elena, I'm just not sure that we can afford to take the risk of pulling some of our top analysts off project efforts. As you know, our funding comes from the revenues of the firm, and they watch very closely on how much of the money allocated to IT goes towards the delivery of business capabilities via projects, and how much is consumed through non-project organizations like Enterprise Architecture."

Elena replied, "But at the same time, if we're still not delivering at the pace they'd like, doesn't something need to change? If you remember back three years, our SOA efforts were stagnant until we actually articulated the behavior we wanted, and established policies to get us there. This is beginning to feel like the funding policies of the business aren't matching the desired behavior they'd like to see."

Andrea said, "That's a good point, and I think we may have some leverage with it. I also have another idea, though. What you are suggesting is needed is a functional breakdown of the business, right? It's a business analysis activity, correct?"

"Yes, that's correct."

"Well, if that's the case, shouldn't the business be involved with that effort? The business has a very different set of rules for how they fund their resources. A much higher percentage of staff is not dedicated toward time-based project activities, and besides, we're going to need their expertise. If they're committing some of their own resources and have skin in the game, we may have an easier time justifying some of our IT resources."

"I would love to have some of the key business strategists involved in the effort. The more we discuss this, the more I see that what we're describing is business architecture. Just as we broke down the technology domain into shared infrastructure and solution-specific components, we need to do the same thing with the business capabilities."

Andrea replied, "I think that the term 'business architecture' will resonate much better with my colleagues than 'functional reference architecture.' It doesn't sound as technical, and the concept of shared capabilities versus specialized capabilities is very easily described through sales and marketing examples. Why don't you take a first pass at a presentation on this? I have a meeting with the right set of stakeholders for this subject in two weeks. Do you think you can have a draft by the end of this week? Then we can fine-tune it the following week."

Elena said, "I'll get right on it. Thanks for your willingness to let me run with this, Andrea. As I mentioned, I really think this change is necessary to keep our efforts going forward, and I'm glad you see it as well. I'll have that draft for you by mid-afternoon on Friday."

Elena developed the presentation, and Andrea was able to convince the business stakeholders that this effort was necessary to keep, and even accelerate their efforts in continuing to reduce their delivery times and improve their agility in leveraging information technology.

Once approved, a team comprised of senior IT analysts, business strategists, business analysts, and some facilitation from an outside firm that specialized in business architecture development was formed. Within three months they were able to generate their first artifacts that could be leveraged within some IT efforts, and after six months, they had completed a draft architecture that covered all domains of the business.

However, there was an unexpected outcome of this effort. After the domains of the business had been identified, a new project went before the IT governance board to request funding. This project, sponsored by the claims department, was striving to modernize much of the claims process. Among the capabilities desired was the ability to send payouts electronically to Advasco's customers. John, a key member of the board, had been following the business domain modeling efforts. One of his employees had been assigned to the business architecture efforts.

During the presentation, John asked the sponsor, "Have you met with the customer account team about this proposal?"

The sponsor replied, "No, I haven't met with them yet."

John then asked, "How about the accounting team?"

The sponsor again replied, "No, I haven't. We've never had to do that before requesting funding."

Andrea asked, "John, what are your concerns?"

John then replied, "Based upon our business architecture, it's clear to me that this project is going to require interaction with at least the Customer and Account services area as well as with Accounting for payouts. My concern is that these groups may have significant work ahead of them to augment their services that this solution may need. If they haven't been approached, we may have either funding or scheduling issues down the road."

Around the table, heads could be seen nodding up and down. After some discussion, it was agreed that the proposed project should review the new business architecture models and engage the appropriate groups that would be involved in the solution. As a result, the effort was split into multiple, independent efforts. The schedule was adjusted to coincide with the normal release schedule of the services needed, minimizing the disruption to existing consumers. Funding was appropriately distributed across each of the efforts in a subsequent meeting, and the IT governance group all agreed that they had a much higher level of confidence that the effort would be successful.

Analysis for SOA

In this chapter, Advasco focused on the analysis side of SOA. While much of the conversation around SOA focuses on technology, it's the analysis effort that actually defines the service. Standard service implementation technologies are a key part of SOA governance, as described in Chapter 2, but when an organization adopts SOA, a very common question is, "How do we build the right services?" While there are certainly incremental gains that can be obtained by standardizing the technologies used to build services, this does not lead to an environment where the "right" services are built, only an environment where services are built the "right" way.

The challenge that Advasco faced was due to the way that analysis typically occurs in most organizations—as part of a project. While there is always some ad hoc analysis that results in an idea for a project, it is usually the case that the initial idea focusing on delivering an end user facing system establishes boundaries that influence all the decisions that follow. Initially, those boundaries are informal as the project is given enough definition for funding purposes, and once funded, the boundaries become more rigid. As a result, even when we are able to break service development out into its own effort separate from any consumer, one consumer likely influenced the initial definition. In presenting that service to other potential consumers, the initial scope sets the context for the conversation, focused on minor adjustments to the scope, rather than on significant additions that were previously not researched, yet still closely related.

As experienced by Advasco, the clear indicator that project analysis is impacting the ability for SOA to deliver on its promises is when the addition of new consumers results in significant changes to the existing services, whether associated with the addition of new capabilities or an overhaul of the existing service. These are signs that inadequate analysis of the domain for the service was done. This isn't meant to imply that a service should never change, as they most certainly will. It should mean, however, that those changes are incremental and evolutionary rather than revolutionary.

SOA governance must play a role in the analysis process to ensure that the "right" services get built, the desired behavior. The question then, however, is what are the people, policies, and processes that can ensure it?

Clearly, the missing piece of the puzzle in the case of Advasco, and in most organizations, is context. Analysis efforts inside of projects, whether it is a service consumer or a service provider, will continue to occur. What can change is the contextual information that is provided to the team engaged in that project analysis. Just as a technology reference architecture based upon service types and service platforms provided context and policies to guide the decisions associated with building services the "right" way, we need similar context and policies to guide the decisions associated with building the "right" services. There are two techniques that are beginning to be used to provide this contextual information: business process analysis and business domain modeling.

Business Process Analysis

Business process analysis has gained in popularity thanks to the introduction of **Business Process Management (BPM)** technology suites. These suites typically include a modeling environment, a simulation tool, an execution engine, and a monitoring and management system. The suite may also include a task management system, necessary for supporting processes with manual activities.

At its heart, BPM suites are driven by a graphical representation of the process, known as the process model. This model is an analysis artifact. It represents a sequence of activities and decisions, both automated and manual, that when executed, perform a key business process. An example of a business process model is shown in the following figure:

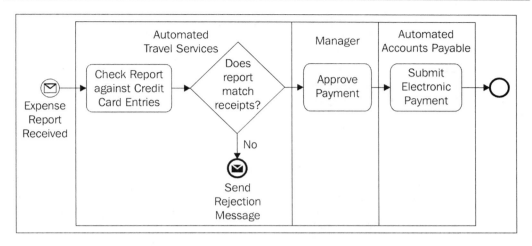

This very simple process is modeled using **Business Process Modeling Notation (BPMN)**. While a thorough discussion of BPMN is outside the scope of this book, this diagram demonstrates the key concepts.

The process starts with the circle on the left. This represents the start event for the process, which in this example, is the receipt of an expense report. The first activity that happens is an automated activity within the **Travel Services** domain, as represented by the encompassing rectangle, known as a swim lane. This activity compares the values in the expense report against the charges reported on the credit card assigned to the submitter. This is represented by the rounded rectangle. If it matches, the report is forwarded to the manager for the submitter for approval. If there are discrepancies, a rejection message is sent back to the submitter and the process is ended. A diamond-shaped box denotes the decision point. The next swim lane represents activities performed by the manager. Within this swim lane there is a single activity of **Approve Payment**. When complete, the next step is an automated activity in the **Accounts Payable** domain, which is to submit an electronic payment to the submitter. Upon completion, the process is ended.

An executable version of this model can be derived, where automated activities are mapped to services in the registry, decision criteria can be mapped to a business rules engine, organizational structure can be imported from an LDAP directory, and more, all maintaining the relationship back to the original analysis model.

At first glance, this model may appear promising. Unlike the traditional application analysis artifacts, this diagram clearly shows where processing spans boundaries. Knowing these boundaries does represent a significant step forward, especially when it includes some information about the organization. The problem, however, is that just as the application analysis artifacts show a view of a single application, the above model shows a view of a single process. In this example, there is only one consumer of a potential electronic payment service. If this service were to be designed based upon the needs described here, there are a number of additional scenarios that could be missed. As an example, it could focus exclusively on electronic payments to employees. In reality, an electronic payment to any number of entities is likely needed.

In our Advasco example, Elena correctly identified this inadequacy in the approach. Just as we needed to go outside the boundaries of the initial project and the initial consumer to define a better service, we also need to go outside the boundaries of the initial process and the initial consumer to define a better service. Simply expanding the boundaries of the project or process may not be enough, since the team may not have any idea how far to expand those boundaries. What is needed is an analysis effort that is independent of any particular project, one that has no boundaries. This effort does not need to perform analysis of the entire enterprise. Its goal should be to perform enough analysis to establish context for the more detailed analysis that will be performed in projects. It is this context that will allow projects to correctly set the boundaries of their analysis efforts.

Business Capability Mapping

In the case of both transitional project and business process analysis techniques, the way to mitigate the risk associated with those efforts was to expand the scope outward. In the case of project analysis, the recommendation was to seek out additional consumers for the services that are identified in the initial analysis efforts. In the case of business process analysis, the same held true, except that the consumers represent additional business processes, rather than additional applications. The question, then, is how can we come up with an analysis artifact that represents this broader view? The artifact that is needed is a business capability map, one that maps services and their associated capabilities to the different business areas and domains.

First, let's look at the view we achieve through traditional functional analysis for an application. We result in a picture that looks like this:

If we expand our scope to other potential consumers that exist, we see that the boundaries of the application must be broken down, allowing services and data to support multiple consumers, as shown in the following diagram:

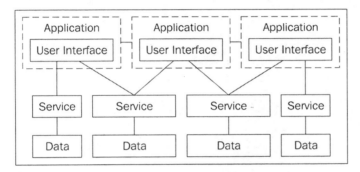

If we do the same thing with a business process approach, we get the following pictures:

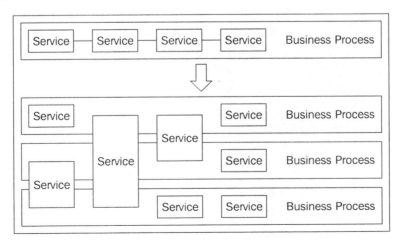

What these the two pictures above demonstrate is that there will be some services that will be shared across one or more applications and one or more business processes. Likewise, there will be some services that will only be used by one process or one application. What we'd like to do is create a view of the services portfolio that gives the analysis team appropriate context to understand the extent to which a service may or may not be shared. Services will come in all shapes and sizes. Some services will be used by one and only one consumer. Some services will be used by many consumers. Some services will be used by other services. Some services will only be shared within a specific business area. We need to provide reference material for analysts that allow them to predict the scope of use for a service.

The other challenge is to provide some context on how to group capabilities into like categories to ensure that services are properly scoped when they are initially identified. While a project will certainly identify one or more capabilities associated with a service, the project, or even the subsequent discussions with other potential consumers, may not reveal the proper scope of capabilities that will constitute the "right" service.

One approach to providing this reference information is to map the capabilities to the business areas. In this approach, a tabular diagram is leveraged to understand the relationship between business areas and capabilities, as shown here:

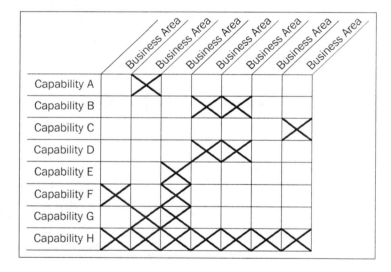

On one dimension are the key business capabilities. These capabilities can have a hierarchical nature, with high level capabilities such as Manufacturing or Order Management decomposing into lower level capabilities such as Inventory Management or Billing, and so on. Some of these lower level capabilities may support multiple higher level capabilities. On the other dimension are the key areas of the business. If that area of the business requires that functional capability, we place an "X" in the cell corresponding to the intersection of the two. The next step is to sort the capabilities by like groupings. If the exact same business areas use two or more capabilities, those capabilities should be ordered together. This allows us to see exactly which capabilities have the potential to be grouped into a common service. Not all capabilities that are in use by the same business areas will necessarily be grouped into a single service. For example, capabilities that are required for all business areas will likely fall into a support area, and it's likely that further specialization can be made within that area to group those capabilities into services.

Another useful way of sorting the rows in the chart is to order them by the number of business areas involved. Items that are only applicable to one business area appear at the top of the list, while items that are broadly applicable appear at the bottom. If we were to draw rectangles around the checked boxes in each row, we wind up with a diagram that looks like this:

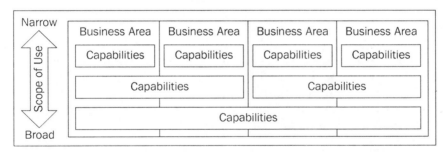

This gives a visual representation of the scope of use for each of the capabilities. This can be beneficial when a project is identified that will create a service that will provide one or more of the capabilities. Prior to seeking out potential consumers, they now have an idea of the breadth of use that is expected.

However, this picture is not complete, because it does not account for areas where an organization may desire to have a redundant implementation of functionality. There is always a tradeoff between the cost savings associated with standardization and the revenue opportunities available to a line of business by pushing new capabilities out quickly. In general, if you want to move as quickly as possible, you need to keep as much of your environment as possible under your own control. When you cross control boundaries, inefficiencies are introduced which slow things up. However, if cost is your primary consideration, the cost savings associated with standardization more than make up for the cost associated with the inefficiencies. If we factor this into the preceding diagram, what we wind up with is a diagram that looks like this:

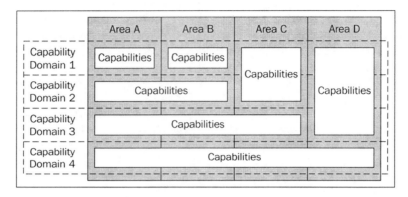

In this diagram, all of the capabilities are grouped into either cells (one set of capabilities, for one business area, within one domain), horizontal blocks (one capability domain, but multiple business areas), or vertical blocks (one business area, but multiple capability domains). Using our Advasco example, the diagram for our example may look something like this:

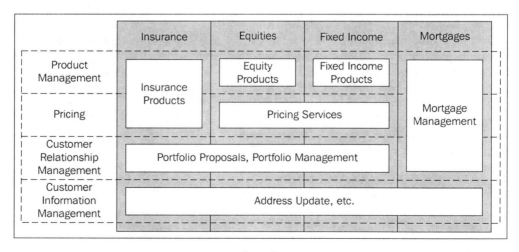

Here we will see how capabilities map across different business areas. At the bottom we see that basic Customer Information Management is a shared capability across the entire organization. However, Customer Relationship Management is not. Advasco may have determined that there is very little crossover between the target customers for their mortgage business versus the rest of their business areas. Likewise, because of the variety of pricing algorithms, the Insurance and Mortgage areas each have their own, tightly integrated systems with the products offered, while equities and fixed income rely on a central pricing engine, but specialized product management capabilities.

This same diagram can be represented in the tabular approach by using color-coding in the cells to denote whether the business area is using a custom solution for the capability or the shared solution. Color coding or shading is recommended over entering a different value in the cell, because a person can very easily pick up the associations by color. For example, if **Capability 3** was shared by **Area A** and **Area D**, we'd have a table that looks like the following:

	Area A	Area B	Area C	Area D
Capability 1				
Capability 2				
Capability 3				
Capability 4				

This can be a very powerful diagram. First, it can be utilized in validating whether the IT landscape matches the corporate governance principles. For example, in the diagram, business **Area D** has its own implementation of the capabilities for all domains except for domain 4. If this business area is one where the company is stressing reduction, the IT landscape is out of alignment with that principle. If this business area is one where the company is emphasizing growth, then this model may be perfectly appropriate.

Another excellent use of this diagram is actually as a current state analysis tool. By surveying the existing application portfolio, documenting their capabilities, and indicating whether they are shared or not, opportunities for strategic services can be more easily identified, especially for systems that may have had no plans for modification in the near horizon.

Business Capability Analysis

However, the natural question that arises from this is, "What are the business capabilities that should be on this chart?" A complete methodology for this is outside the scope of this book, but there are certainly techniques available. Top-down approaches include value chain analysis based on the work of Michael Porter in his 1985 book, *Competitive Advantage: Creating and Sustaining Superior Performance.* Wikipedia, as of June 2008, provides the following definition of value chains and value chain analysis (`http://en.wikipedia.org/w/index.php?title=Value_ chain&oldid=215039258`):

> *"A value chain is a chain of activities. Products pass through all activities of the chain in order and at each activity the product gains some value. The chain of activities gives the products more added value than the sum of added values of all activities. It is important not to mix the concept of the value chain with the costs occurring throughout the activities. A diamond cutter can be used as an example of the difference. The cutting activity may have a low cost, but the activity adds too much of the value of the end product, since a rough diamond is significantly less valuable than a cut diamond.*
>
> *The value chain categorizes the generic value-adding activities of an organization. The "primary activities" include: inbound logistics, operations (production), outbound logistics, marketing and sales (demand), and services (maintenance). The "support activities" include: administrative infrastructure management, human resource management, information technology, and procurement. The costs and value drivers are identified for each value activity. The value chain framework quickly made its way to the forefront of management thought as a powerful analysis tool for strategic planning. Its ultimate goal is to maximize value creation while minimizing costs."*

Likewise, many professional services organizations have methodologies that focus exclusively on the analysis side of SOA. IBM Global Services has a methodology called **Service Oriented Modeling and Architecture**, or **SOMA** for short. Another resource available is the Capgemini Methodology for Service Architectures, which was released into the public domain in 2005 as part of the OASIS SOA Adoption Blueprints effort (`http://www.oasis-open.org/committees/download. php/15071/A%20methodology%20for%20Service%20Architectures%201%202%20 4%20-%20OASIS%20Contribution.pdf`). Both of these efforts also include additional models that provide similar information to the business capability mapping described earlier, such as the use of heat maps.

Finally, there are some industry standard capability models that are available, such as the ACORD efforts in the insurance industry, or the OTA efforts in the travel and leisure industries. Many of these efforts go beyond simple standard data definitions and delve into capabilities and services that are standard across the industry where they apply.

The end goal of these analysis techniques is to produce reference material for use in the governance of SOA. To that end, any of the analysis methodologies and artifacts must provide the following:

- A list of business capabilities and their relation to other capabilities in the organization
- A categorization of these capabilities by their purpose in the organization
- An alignment of capabilities to organizational unit responsible for the delivery of those capabilities

With these three key elements an organization can provide the necessary reference information for their project-based analysis efforts.

Project Inception Checkpoints

So how are these artifacts used for governance? In Chapter 3 we discussed the existing governance process within the project lifecycle. While many of these artifacts can, and should, be used as part of the analysis phase, funding has already been allocated to the project, which puts pressure on the team to constrain scope, rather than getting the scope right.

The correct time to initially incorporate this reference material is during the inception phase of an effort, prior to requesting formal funding. As part of determining the scope and the cost of the work that will be completed, the team putting together the proposal should be reviewing the reference material, just as a technical architecture should be reviewing reference architecture before proposing a solution architecture. You don't propose a project until you've reviewed the contextual information of how projects should be defined.

The Service Registry/Repository also plays a key role in facilitating the proper behavior. As mentioned earlier, the models can be filled in based upon current state analysis. Doing so can identify opportunities for consolidation of multiple implementations into a single implementation. If these opportunities have been identified, these services can be entered into the Service Registry/Repository with a status of "Desired" or "Proposed." If this is done, a team putting together a project proposal can review the Service Registry/Repository to see if their proposed capabilities overlap with any desired or proposed service, and if so, their scope and funding demand can be augmented appropriately.

Therefore, augmenting the previous discussed checkpoints, the Project Inception checkpoint should answer the following questions:

- Has the project identified potential services that it may require?
- Has each potential service been mapped back to the business capability map?
- Has the scope for each potential service been properly defined according to the business capability map?
- Has the responsible business area for the potential services been identified and contacted for the purposes of defining scope and funding?
- Have existing systems been taken into account as potential service providers for the purposes of defined scope and funding?
- Is all usage of shared services justified according to the current business capability map?
- Is all usage of dedicated services justified according to the current business capability map?
- Does the funding reflect the appropriate scope for the capabilities desired according to the business capability map?
- Does the proposed schedule for the effort reflect the normal release cycles for any existing services?
- Has the sequence of delivery of services and consumers been appropriately defined to allow for key services to be developed well in advance of consumer demand?

Summary

In this chapter, Advasco had progressed past their initial success and were now experiencing some challenges. The state in which they were operating was best described as just-in-time. Despite successful efforts to manage the service lifecycle, new things kept coming along within projects that challenged the way that existing services had been defined. Service providers would need to react just-in-time, since the project had already been funded and had deadlines that needed to be met.

Analysis of the situation by the Center of Excellence, the Chief Architect, and a team of key service managers determined that the root cause was the fact that all analysis discussions around the scope of services did not occur until after the project had been funded and started. As a result, the approved scope of the project had an impact on all subsequent discussions. Surprisingly, even when the service teams had subsequent meetings with other consumers, the requirements of the initial consumer that identified the service still influenced the discussion and scope definition of the service.

When looking at the analysis methods in use, the team recognized that both the traditional functional analysis used on projects, as well as the newer business process analysis techniques associated with BPM suites, both had risks of being short-sighted in their scope because they were focused on a single project or a single process. The team chose to form a business architecture team that could perform analysis outside of the context of any particular project or process. This team mapped the desired business capabilities back to the key business areas and these artifacts were included as part of the governance process that is required to achieve funding for projects. As a result, many projects had their scope, schedule, and funding augmented prior to approval to ensure that the "right" services were built.

The key to success is the establishment of an effort that allows analysis to be performed outside of the context of any particular project, and as such, is not overly influenced by the needs of any one particular system or department. Existing functional analysis artifacts, including business process models and traditional functional analysis artifacts, are inputs to the process. The analysis artifact to be produced by this effort must represent a mapping of business capabilities to the areas in need of those services. Where a business capability maps to a single business area, ownership and usage is very clear. Where a business capability spans multiple business areas, ownership must be determined. Business capabilities that are desired by the same business areas should be investigated for possible aggregation into a single service, managed by a single team. It is not required for all business capabilities to have a single implementation that is used across the organization, but where multiple implementations exist, the decision to do so must be consistent with the organization's goals for the business areas involved. A strategy for cost reduction does not justify having multiple implementations of the same capability.

In order to determine the set of capabilities desired, organizations can take a top-down approach, such as value chain analysis, or any of the many methodologies for SOA analysis available from professional services organizations. Likewise, a bottom-up approach can be used. In this approach, the existing portfolio of applications is reviewed to document the capabilities associated with them. This may yield new opportunities across applications that may presently be in a maintenance mode without plans for any significant modifications that would require taking a deep look at their current capabilities.

This mapping of capabilities to business areas should be leveraged as part of the project inception process, where there normally is a governance checkpoint focused on establishing funding for the effort. Policies that reflect the desired behavior to build the "right" services must be enforced at this time to get the organization out of the habit of "just-in-time" change and onto the path of strategic service development.

6

Governing Run-Time Behavior

SOA Governance in the run-time environment needs to go beyond security and versioning. As many as possible aspects of the run-time behavior between a consumer and a provider should be expressed in the service contract and enforced by the run-time infrastructure. The team at Advasco will learn exactly what can happen when these aspects are not captured in policies and not enforced by the run-time infrastructure.

Preparing for Partner Services

"Tomorrow is the big day, isn't it Maria?" asked Spencer.

"Yes, it's great to finally make our services available to our agency partners. We've had so much success with our use of services internally; it's exciting to be opening them up to our partners and making it easier for them to do business with us. I know many of the independent agents have choices on whose financial products they want to market. Anything we do that improves our image in their minds can help our business," said Maria.

"Did you run into any challenges during the testing phase?" asked Spencer.

"No, I'd say things went very smoothly. All of our partners were able to execute transactions successfully. We had a few challenges trying to get the mappings right between the messaging standards and our own internal formats, but that's normal for these types of services."

"How did your performance tests go?"

"All of the tests went well. We had a good idea on the expected load based upon the analysis of the existing transactions that we execute through our legacy interfaces. We even ran tests that included our own internal use of the same services, as well as some typical traffic for services that leverage the same infrastructure. Everything looks good."

"Sounds great. Well good luck. I'm sure everything will go off without a hitch. Your team has a great track record."

True to form, everything did go off without a hitch. Everyone was on edge for the first day as traffic started to flow through the system, but no errors were encountered on the first day, the first week, or even the first month. Agency partners began using the services on a staggered schedule, and all had completed their integration by the end of two months.

Ed, an analyst on Maria's team, had the responsibility of checking the usage reports for the services. These reports contained some basic information, simply showing the number of requests a service had received, the number of requests that succeeded/ failed, the average response time, and the average message size. As the number of requests increased over time, the average response time for the service had remained consistent. There was the normal variability from day to day, but the running average was 650ms. During the first month, Ed was religious about monitoring the performance of the services. Over the second month, however, because things had gone so smoothly and because his other responsibilities were competing for his time, Ed began to monitor the usage reports less frequently. At the end of the second month, Ed hadn't reviewed the reports for over two weeks. However, he knew that all of the agency partners had completed their integration, so he wasn't surprised at all to see that the number of requests per day had increased significantly. The average response time was still around 650ms, so he thought nothing of it.

However, what Ed hadn't noticed was that the number of requests had already exceeded the capacity levels that were tested during the performance testing of the service. Ed hadn't been involved in that effort, so he wasn't aware that the existing behavior was outside of the norm. Furthermore, his instructions in monitoring the service in production were only to ensure that we reacted quickly when something went wrong. There were alerts in place that would notify him if the service stopped responding.

For the next week, Ed reviewed the daily reports, knowing that all consumers were now using the service. The average response time continued to remain steady. There was an increase in the number of requests each day, but he attributed this to the normal fluctuations of the business. After the first week, Ed stopped reviewing the reports, putting his faith in the automated alerts. This would prove to be a mistake.

The First Sign of Trouble

Three weeks later, Andrea called Maria on the phone. "Maria, are you aware of any problems with the services in use by our agency partners? I just received a phone call from our agency relations manager telling me that they're experiencing poor performance from our services."

This caught Maria off guard. "I'm sorry Andrea, but this is the first I've heard of any problems. I know we have monitoring in place to detect if the services are unavailable, but I haven't heard of any alerts from it. I'll get right on it and talk to Ed and see what our reports are saying."

Andrea replied, "Thanks Maria. Please let me know as soon as you find something so I can get back with the manager."

Maria immediately called Ed and asked, "Ed, have you seen any anomalies in our agency services? I just got a call from Andrea that said some of our partner agencies have been complaining about poor performance."

Ed said, "Umm…. Let me go into the service management console and pull up the latest report. I haven't looked at them in a while since things had been going so well."

Maria was already concerned after hearing this. She had expected that Ed was looking at these reports every single day. Admittedly, however, she too had been guilty of ignoring many of the usage reports she received by email after her services had been in production for a significant length of time.

"Whoa."

"What do you mean, 'whoa?' That doesn't make me feel comfortable, Ed."

"Our average response time is about three times what it was three weeks ago," he replied.

"Are we seeing any failures?"

"No, I'm not showing any failed requests, just some which are taking quite a long time to execute. Let me check with operations and see if the application server cluster hosting these services has been rebooted recently. I know from past experience that those services can start to behave strangely if they're not rebooted every now and then."

Ed checked with operations, and sure enough, the application servers hadn't been restarted since the service went live three months ago. He scheduled a change request for that night to bounce the servers and let Maria know.

Maria passed this information back to Andrea, "We did see that the average response time for the service went up significantly over the past three weeks. No requests failed, which is why we didn't receive any monitoring alerts. Ed checked into it, and determined that the application servers hosting the service had not been bounced since the service went live. We've scheduled that change for tonight, and hopefully it will fix the problem."

"Thanks for digging into this, Maria. Keep a close eye on things tomorrow."

Day Two

The server bounce was completed as scheduled, and Ed immediately started watching the usage reports when he arrived in the morning. Unfortunately, after the first hour of usage, things didn't appear any better. By 10:00am he knew that the problem was still there and called Maria.

"Maria, it looks like our server reboot didn't fix the problem. I've watched the first two hours of data from today, and the response time is still pretty poor. Perhaps the problem is somewhere in a back-end dependency."

"Thanks for keeping a close eye on things, Ed. Rally the people that you need to look into the dependent systems and let me know what you're able to find out. I'll advise Andrea."

Maria notified Andrea that the problem wasn't fixed by the reboot and asked her to make sure that the Agency Relations manager was aware, in case more phone calls came in.

In the meantime, Ed had gathered together the operations staff responsible for monitoring the database system and the mainframe components that the services utilized. He explained the situation to them and asked them to research their logs and determine if their systems were performing as expected.

Unfortunately, it wasn't an easy task to determine whether these systems were behaving properly for the requests associated with these services. Both the mainframe and the database system were used by many other systems. The operations team promised to do their best, but told Ed that they couldn't pull the logs, perform the appropriate filtering and analysis, and get the data until the end of the day.

Around 5:30pm the operations team got back to him, and unfortunately, Ed was no closer to an answer than he was at the beginning of the day. If anything, he was more confused about what was going on. From the perspective of the database and mainframe, everything was performing as expected. They had not found any signs of problems within the database or the mainframe. All indications concluded that the systems were performing normally.

Ed stayed up very late trying to determine what the root cause of the problem was; however, unfortunately, he didn't come up with any answers. He left late that night after sending Maria an email letting her know that he was no closer to solving the problem. The good news was that they still had not recorded any failures, but the response time for the services had increased again today and Ed knew that sooner or later that response time would cause problems.

Day Three

Ed didn't sleep well that night, knowing that another day of searching for the root cause of the problem lied ahead. He made sure to get a venti latte from Starbucks on his way in, knowing he'd need the extra caffeine to keep him going.

He called together the operations team that had been helping him first thing in the morning, and decided to start from scratch.

"Team, as you know, the performance of our services that support our agency partners has been degrading, and it's rapidly getting worse. We've rebooted our application servers, and checked our dependencies on the mainframe and database, both of which checked out okay. I'd like your thoughts on where else to look. Another set of eyes may help point something out that I haven't noticed."

Sarah, from the middleware monitoring group asked, "What do these services do? Is there any chance that some bad code could be causing the problem?"

Ed said, "I know the team did significant performance tests before going into production. I think any bad code would have been caught by that testing effort."

Alex, from the Linux team, asked, "What does the CPU look like on the application servers? Perhaps some of the XML processing is chewing up CPU and slowing things down."

Ed replied, "I've checked that as well, and I didn't see anything out of the norm. That's what is so strange. Based upon CPU load, and the data from the database systems and the mainframe, we shouldn't be seeing this behavior."

Sarah suddenly got a thought. "Ed, this sounds very familiar to a debugging scenario I had back when we had issues with our messaging infrastructure. In that case, we were building up backlogs of messages to be processed. When we looked at data from points where processing was occurring, everything looked normal. It was only when we looked at the incoming message traffic that we determined we had a bottleneck. Have you looked at the number of requests being processed to see if there's something strange there?"

While Sarah didn't intend any ill will, Ed felt like a fool. He had not reviewed the number of requests that had been flowing through the system. Ed sheepishly said, "I can't believe I haven't looked at that. Let's bring up the reports."

Ed quickly brought up the management console, and there, in black and white, was some glaring information. Traffic had been steadily increasing every single day to the point where the system was now trying to handle ten times the traffic for which it was designed.

Sarah said, "Well, it looks like we know the source of the problem. The real question is what do we do about it?"

Alex replied, "Would it help if we added some additional servers to the farm for these services?"

Ed said, "Unfortunately, I think that's a temporary fix. We need to figure out where all of this additional traffic is coming from."

Alex suggested, "Can we capture a sample of the incoming requests to determine that?"

Ed said, "Our service management infrastructure may already have that information for us. Let me dig deeper into the reporting console and see what I can find out."

Back on the management console, Ed was disappointed when he saw that the default reporting that was enabled could only show aggregate information across all of the consumers. However, all was not lost because Ed knew that every service request contained a unique identifier that indicated the source of the request. This had become a requirement for all service messages back when Advasco dealt with versioning for the first time. It was simply a matter of instructing the service management system to index its data based upon this message element. Ed configured the platform to do so, and then waited for the results.

Within the next hour, Ed had already collected enough data to determine which consumer was flooding the system with requests. He let Maria know, and she immediately went to the Service Registry/Repository to determine the point-of-contact for that consumer, since it was an external partner. The partner was notified and began researching its own systems in the meantime; they agreed to disable their consuming application from sending service requests until the root cause was identified. Advasco was lucky this time. The partner disabled their consuming application only because it was not deemed to be mission critical, and their business could withstand not using it for a few days until the problem had been corrected. Had this been a business critical application, turning it off may not have been an option.

Day Four

The next day, Ed arrived far better rested than the previous morning. His pager didn't go off at all overnight. He reviewed the reports for the service usage, including his more detailed breakdown by consumer, and was pleased to see that there were no additional problems once access from the offending partner had been disabled.

He gave Maria the good news, "Maria, it looks like we've resolved the problem. Once the consumer who was flooding our system was disabled, things suddenly started to work better. I've reviewed the reports since that change was made, and we are well under the capacity levels for which the system was designed."

"That's great news Ed. However, my bigger concern now is how do we prevent it from happening again?"

"We should have some answers for you later this afternoon. I'm on my way to meet with the SOA Center of Excellence to discuss exactly that topic."

"Let me know what the recommendation is as soon as you know."

In the meeting, Spencer started things off, "Thanks for joining us Ed. As we get started, I want to remind everyone that our purpose here is to figure out how we can prevent this from happening again, not to dwell on activities that did or did not occur that led to the problems. Ed, can you give us a brief walkthrough of what the root cause was determined to be?"

Ed proceeded to inform the COE that the performance degradation was directly attributable to a continuously increasing load from one consumer. Because the operations involved were all read-only, the requests went unnoticed until they reached a level that started impacting other operations.

Jared asked the question, "Do we know what kind of testing was done by our partners? It seems that this should have been caught during one of our performance tests."

Raj replied, "I don't know if that would have caught the problem. The partner that caused the problem was in production for over three weeks. Even when we've run long running capacity tests that accelerated the pace of requests, we've never run something that would have simulated three weeks' worth of activity."

Spencer then asked, "I know we did our own internal capacity testing based upon numbers from the web application many of the partners previously used. Did we have that request data broken down by partner, or did we only have aggregate data?"

Ed replied, "It's my understanding that we only had aggregate data available to us."

Spencer added, "That's unfortunate. I don't know that there's much we could have done to prevent this situation except to go to a completely asynchronous invocation model. Given that the majority of the operations are read-only, I don't know that our partners would have accepted that."

Jared replied, "If we had the data broken down by consumer, would that have helped?"

Spencer said, "Remember our debate around service versioning? We had some good discussions about policy-driven infrastructure, and I think we've just found another area where it can be applied. While I know we can't control the logic of our partners' applications, we can take some actions to ensure the integrity of our systems and the availability of our services to other partners. As it stands right now, our services are out there for our partners to do whatever they want. We don't bill by the invocation, rather we get revenue indirectly through the policies they sell. It's unrealistic for them to think we can handle whatever bad code they may have written. How many of you have cable modems at home for broadband access?"

About two-thirds of the COE raised their hands. "Raj, what happens if you start doing some peer-to-peer transfers to give your latest home videos to your extended family? Does your cable company let you consume all of the bandwidth for your neighborhood? No, they throttle it. I think we need to do the same thing here. The only missing piece is the levels at which we throttle things."

Ed replied, "I don't know that any of our partners would be happy if some of their requests were throttled."

Spencer replied, "The message we need to deliver is that our intent is not to throttle normal use of the system, or even slightly above normal use. What we want to do is ensure that significantly abnormal use is detected and dealt with appropriately to ensure the integrity and availability of the system for all of our consumers."

Jared asked, "How do we go about determining what 'normal' behavior is?"

Spencer replied, "It really should just be an extension of the same mechanisms we used to determine the original capacity. Furthermore, it should be a conversation between each partner individually. We have some partners that are going to generate significantly more traffic than others, and that should be taken into account."

Ed asked, "But what if this was a brand new service where we didn't have any reference data to draw from?"

Spencer replied, "How would we go about determining the initial capacity? If we don't have some kind of numbers, we're at risk of running out of capacity without any consumer having bad code. We simply need to do the analysis that we already should be doing anyway."

Raj stated, "I think this approach will work. We just need to extend the existing service contracts to include anticipated usage information which includes thresholds that are tied back to specific notifications. The first threshold may result in a warning message being sent to the partner POC, while the second threshold would result in messages being rejected."

Jared said, "I agree with that approach. The analysis that occurs during the development lifecycle should establish the initial baseline for the expected behavior. This can then be refined after some time in production, and thresholds can be adjusted accordingly."

Spencer said, "The way you two describe it, it sounds like this is something that should be handled by our XML appliances, much in the same way we're dealing with security policies and versioning policies. Ed, is this something you can look into?"

Ed replied, "Well, my job is more focused on monitoring the environment, but I work closely with the team responsible for engineering the environment. They should know whether or not this could be handled by the infrastructure. I'll contact them and get back to you as soon as possible."

After the meeting, Ed went by to see Sarah from the middleware monitoring group. That group was also responsible for the XML appliances. "Sarah, thanks for your help in our troubleshooting effort. I have another question for you."

"Sure, Ed. What's your question?" she replied.

"It turns out that the problems were caused by one of our partners slowly flooding our system with service requests, probably due to a bug in their code. The COE has asked that we look into the capabilities of the XML appliances in enforcing policies on the request rate allowed on a per consumer basis. Is this something you can help me with?"

"I'd be glad to help you out, Ed. Let me clear it with my manager, but I don't expect that it will be a problem."

Testing the Solution

After researching the capabilities of the XML appliance, Ed and Sarah felt confident that it could do what they desired, although some adjustments had to be made. The biggest hurdle was that two appliances were used within the external gateway, but they normally didn't communicate with each other. The challenge this posed is that a client that sends 1,000 requests per hour may have 500 go to one appliance and 500 go to the other appliance. If the threshold was set at 1,000 requests per hour on each appliance, theoretically, a client could actually send 2,000 requests per hour, if requests were equally balanced in load across the two appliances. If the threshold was set at 500 requests per hour on each appliance, there is a risk that requests could be throttled when the client was still below the 1,000 requests per hour rate and their requests were not balanced across the two appliances equally.

After some debate, Ed and Sarah took a slightly different path. Rather than having immediate enforcement at the appliance, they chose to have the policy enforced via the analytics engine on the management server. This engine received metric information from each appliance, correlating the information. It could then analyze the true rate of requests across all appliances and take action if thresholds were exceeded. In this case, the action was to invoke a service on the management console itself that would update policies on the appliances to reject requests for the consumer whose SLA was violated for a configurable time period. At the end of the time period, the policies would be restored back.

They then executed their tests with two consumers, one that maintained a steady rate of requests, and one that had a steadily increasing rate of requests. They first verified that without any throttling policies, the consumer with the stable rate of requests would eventually see performance degradation as the rate of requests increased from the other consumer, replicating the behavior that was seen in the production.

A policy for throttling requests was then established based upon the rate of requests that caused the performance degradation to begin. Two thresholds were established. Exceeding the first threshold simply resulted in an email notification being sent to the POC associated with the consumer, violating the second threshold resulted in subsequent requests being rejected until the rate of usage in the moving window dropped back below the threshold. Throttling levels were then assigned to each consumer and the test was re-run.

The test was successful. The consumer with the stable rate of requests (which was below both thresholds) never saw any degradation of performance. The consumer with the ever-increasing rate of requests was notified successfully via email when the first threshold was reached, and requests were rejected for a time period when the second threshold was reached.

The results of these tests were communicated back to the COE, and then back to Maria. Maria worked with the Partner Relations manager to determine how to implement the solution. Meetings were held with each partner to establish the baseline usage, the warning threshold, and the rejection threshold. Baselines were based upon production usage to date.

Once the partners modified their code to take appropriate action based upon the receipt of a rejected request, the changes were implemented. While the partner that caused the problem that set the chain events off had found and fixed their bug, the experience brought light to the importance of daily monitoring and analysis of trends. Both the partners and Advasco began making associations between the usage characteristics and the context of the time periods measured that proved very valuable to their businesses and to the ability of operations to properly manage the environment. Thankfully, none of the partners ever had any requests rejected in production, although the policies came in handy in the test environments when some of the partners' testing scripts had some bugs in them.

Run-Time SOA Governance and the Service Contract

In Chapter 2 the concept of the service contract was first introduced. The focus was on the functional interface, and the delivery schedule for the service implementation. In Chapter 4 the contract was extended to contain versioning information. By specifying the version of the service interface associated with a particular client, transformations and routing rules can be put in place to facilitate having multiple versions of a service implementation in production and ease the timeframe in which consumers must migrate.

In this chapter the focus is on the rest of the run-time behavior of the systems. Once again, remember that governance is about people, policies, and processes that are put in place to achieve the desired behavior. In the example in this chapter, the desired behavior for the run-time environment had not been established, nor had policies been created to ensure any implied behavior.

Based upon the reactions of the Advasco staff, one could infer that the desired behavior for the run-time environment was:

- Ensure consistent performance of services for all consumers
- Ensure that no one consumer can prevent other consumers from accessing services
- Detect problems before they are reported by consumers

The first potential problem is when the desired behaviors are not explicitly specified. We inferred desired behavior from the actions of the staff. Therefore, the first step in establishing run-time SOA governance is no different than it was for the general SOA adoption effort: define your desired behavior. Once this has been done, the next step is to have the appropriate people establish the policies that will lead to the desired behavior. Once again, in our example, this step had not been taken. From Ed's failure to review the metrics everyday, to the failure of the infrastructure to prevent an individual consumer from flooding the system with requests, there were potential areas where policies could have encouraged the correct behavior.

Ensuring Consistent Performance

In order to ensure consistent performance of services for all consumers, what are the policies that are needed? While Advasco did not explicitly specify their policies, we can again infer some best practices by analyzing the activities that took place when the services were first moved into production. As with most systems, a significant amount of attention is given when they first go live, and the attention goes down over time. What is preferable is to establish a standard for monitoring that applies regardless of whether it's the first day in production or the fiftieth day in production. The activities of Advasco on day one led to the following policies:

- The performance of each service must be monitored and reviewed no less than once per business day.
- Metrics must be collected for all services at all times.

Metric Collection

Metric collection is clearly the linchpin of any effort to govern run-time behavior, so additional policies are needed around them. In addition to the daily aggregated information, Advasco was able to see real-time information when they were in debugging mode. Once again, the metric collection behavior should be expressed in terms of policies:

- Aggregated metrics must be available at five minute, 15 minute, and hourly intervals.
- Aggregated metrics at less than one hour intervals must be available for up to seven days.
- Aggregated metrics at one-hour intervals or greater must be available indefinitely.
- Raw metrics for individual service requests must be available for one day.

- Metrics must be sortable by:
    - ° Service requested (across all consumers)
    - ° Operation requested (across all consumers)
    - ° Consumer (all service requests from a single consumer)
    - ° Consumer type (for example, internal versus external)
    - ° Time of day
    - ° Any combination of the above

The exact aggregation intervals will vary by company, the important part is to have them explicitly specified and expressed as policy. Keeping in mind the concept of policy-driven infrastructure, a change in policy should be quick to implement. Therefore, if an organization wanted to change the aggregation intervals, this should be something easily done in the matter of minutes or hours, rather than days or weeks. In choosing the aggregation intervals, the organization must be sensitive to the storage required for the metrics. While it may be possible to store raw metrics for every single service request for one day when an organization is only processing a few million each day, an organization that processes hundreds of millions of requests may not have that luxury.

The last policy in the list is also one of key importance. Simply recording a timestamp and a response time for a request yields good information, but it also ignores even more. An organization must examine the metadata that will be stored with each record. Items that should be considered for service requests are:

- Time request was received
- Source IP address of request
- Identity of requester (as represented on the message, such as a user identifier)
- Identity of consumer (should be different from user identifier, such as a system identifier or company identifier)
- URL requested
- Service requested
- Operation requested
- Size of the request
- Unique identifier (can be generated by the infrastructure)
- One or more attributes extracted from message payload

For the last item, it can be useful to reserve elements in the metric record for customization by individual service owners. While capturing the entire payload can be valuable in debugging, it does not lend itself well to searching and indexing, in addition to potentially taking up large amounts of storage. Instead, key attributes from the message can be extracted via XPath or XQuery expressions and stored as indexed attributes in the metric record. For example, if a service request looked like this:

```
<soap:Envelope xmlns:soap="http://schemas.xmlsoap.org/soap/envelope/"
xmlns:xsi="http://www.w3.org/2001/XMLSchema-instance" xmlns:s="http://
www.w3.org/2001/XMLSchema" xmlns:tns="http://www.advasco.com/">
 <soap:Header>
   <wsse:Security xmlns:wsse="http://docs.oasis-open.org/wss/2004/01/
oasis-200401-wss-wssecurity-secext-1.0.xsd">
     <wsu:Timestamp xmlns:wsu="http://docs.oasis-open.org/wss/2004/01/
oasis-200401-wss-wssecurity-utility-1.0.xsd" wsu:Id="Timestamp-
aaddaaf5-1207-44d7-a5ab-64b6bf5f678e">
       <wsu:Created>2008-05-27T21:23:25Z</wsu:Created>
     </wsu:Timestamp>
     <wsse:UsernameToken xmlns:wsu="http://docs.oasis-open.org/
wss/2004/01/oasis-200401-wss-wssecurity-utility-1.0.xsd" wsu:
Id="SecurityToken-53f28e17-d945-4966-aef1-3ab95e680721">
       <wsse:Username>jdoe</wsse:Username>
       <wsse:Password Type="http://docs.oasis-open.org/wss/2004/01/
oasis-200401-wss-username-token-profile-1.0#PasswordDigest">2gy4KlZvot
tIW989aDMD6JTL/Mk=</wsse:Password>
       <wsse:Nonce>EqJ39Y6g6V+X9XgLIwx1Wg==</wsse:Nonce>
       <wsu:Created>2008-05-27T21:23:25Z</wsu:Created>
     </wsse:UsernameToken>
   </wsse:Security>
   <tns:Consumer>
     <tns:SystemId>PolicyEntry</tns:SystemId>
   </tns:Consumer>
 </soap:Header>
 <soap:Body>
   <tns:GetCustomer>
    <tns:customer-id>abc123</tns:customer-id>
   </tns:GetCustomer>
 </soap:Body>
</soap:Envelope>
```

to extract the identity of the consumer from this message, the following XPath expression would be used:

```
string(/soap:Envelope/soap:Header/tns:Consumer/tns:SystemId)
```

For service responses, a similar set of attributes should be examined:

- Time that the response was received
- The IP address that the response was sent from
- The identity of the requester (as represented on the message, such as a user identifier)
- The identity of the consumer (should be different from the user identifier, such as a system identifier or company identifier)
- URL associated with response
- Service endpoint associated with response
- Operation associated with response
- Size of the response message
- Unique identifier
- Message ID of the request (for correlation to the original request)
- One or more attributes extracted from the request message
- One or more attributes extracted from the response message

Finally, for reporting purposes, you need to consider how to efficiently associate information that wasn't contained on individual messages with the metric information. For example, while an individual message will contain the identity of the consumer, it won't necessarily tell you if that consumer is an external consumer or an internal consumer. This information is likely contained in a service registry/repository, where the relationship between consumers and providers is maintained. Joining the two at the time the report is generated may not be easy to do, depending on the tools involved.

Preventing Consumer Starvation

Looking at the second component of the desired behavior, what are the policies that will ensure that no one consumer can prevent other consumers from accessing services? The two policies that Advasco chose to adopt and enforce were:

- Consumers must be notified when service usage exceeds a threshold where continued usage at that rate can impact the availability to other consumers.
- Service requests from a particular consumer must be rejected when the usage rate from that consumer exceeds a threshold, jeopardizing the stability of the service and its availability to other consumers.

Of course, the natural question is what are the thresholds? Therefore, there were two additional policies that Advasco adopted:

- All consumers must establish a usage threshold for each service used that, when exceeded, will result in the consumer's POC being notified.

- All consumers must establish a usage threshold for each service, higher than the notification threshold, that when exceeded, will result in service requests from that consumer being rejected.

This leads to a discussion on expected versus unexpected behavior. It is very difficult to implement any of these policies unless there is an idea on what the expected behavior is. To do this, these additional policies for service consumers are needed:

- A service consumer must provide a baseline characterization of service utilization prior to any production usage.

- A baseline characterization must include enough information to adequately describe normal behavior and easily distinguish abnormal behavior when reviewing actual metrics.

The phrasing on the second policy is the key. Often times, organizations may tell groups that they need to provide the expected number of requests per hour or day, but this may not be the right way to capture normal behavior. For example, there may be financial applications in the enterprise that are only run at the end of the month, quarter, or year. Trying to express their baseline characterization of service utilization on a daily basis doesn't make sense, as most days will have zero utilization, while other days there may be hundreds of thousands of requests sent. At the same time, it is important that this utilization be expressed in a manner that allows the infrastructure to provide automated monitoring wherever possible.

Service consumers are not the only ones that must provide a definition of expected behavior. Service providers must also characterize their behavior, leading to the following policies:

- A service provider must provide a baseline characterization of service performance prior to any production usage.

- The baseline characterization must include enough information to adequately describe normal behavior and easily distinguish abnormal behavior when reviewing actual metrics.

- A service provider must provide a baseline available capacity, based upon the configuration of the infrastructure at the time of deployment.

- Baseline performance and available capacity must be updated whenever changes to the underlying service implementation and associated platform are made.

Characterizing normal behavior from the standpoint of the service provider is a bit different. While service consumers are focused on providing information on how they will use services, service providers should be focused on describing information on how resources are utilized when a service is used. A service consumer cannot, and should not, have any idea of the CPU or memory utilization associated with the processing of its service requests, but it certainly should have an idea regarding how many requests it will typically send, and when it will send them. A service provider, on the other hand, absolutely should understand how CPU and memory is utilized when service requests or processed, but it is up to the service consumers to define when those resources are actually utilized.

Defining Service Consumer Baselines

In the case of service consumers, initial baselines are established through analysis, rather than formal testing. For example, if the service consumer is a web application, the team should be able to characterize the interaction that a typical user may have. By looking at the individual web pages that are requested, the team can inspect the code to determine the number of services requested associated with the processing on each of those pages. By multiplying by the number of simultaneous users on the system, and any variation in the rate of usage, the service utilization can be characterized. Factors that should be looked at include:

- Will the application be used as part of normal daily processing, or is it associated with particular business events, such as the end of a financial reporting period?

- Is the application used by home users or by business users? If the former, a higher utilization may occur during evening and weekends, while the latter may see usage within the hours of 8am to 5pm, Monday to Friday.

- Is the application utilized in a particular region, or is it deployed globally? Are there any differences in the size of user population according to the region? These questions will determine whether or not the application experiences periods of low utilization during the day, or if a sustained load is seen over the entire day.

- Is the application used as a part of processing revenue producing activities, such as placing financial transactions, or is it primarily used in support of business activities, such as updating address information. Often times, support activities take place when people "have time". In the financial services industry in the United States, many of the support activities are done outside of the hours in which trading markets are open. As a result, a spike of activity for support applications can occur when the office is open, but the trading markets are closed, and during the lunch hour.

- Is the system replacing some other system or technique for performing the same purpose? For example, if an organization is exposing business-to-business services for accepting orders that is complimentary to an existing web-based application for the same purpose, it can reasonably assume that the amount of orders processed via the service interface will be similar to the number of orders processed via the web application.

Upfront analysis is very critical to ensuring the success of the system at launch, but baselines determined from actual utilization ultimately will be a more valuable metric. This is why many organizations leverage analysis and research firms that collect data from actual utilization measurements from other companies doing similar activities in forming their upfront baselines. This leads to additional policies for governing the run-time environment:

- Consumers must update their expected utilization baseline based upon an analysis of actual measurements from production after the system has been rolled out to the full user population and time allowed for initial learning.
- Whenever business events or the business climate changes, the baseline utilization must be adjusted to account for the change.

What these policies state is that the baseline is not a set of metrics that are established once and then ignored. The baseline must be continually refined as part of the lifecycle of the service consumer. Clearly, the first event is the rollout of the service consumer in production and the adoption by the end users. However, other business events will continually modify this. For example, suppose a company has retail locations or branch offices, and some of the service consumers are systems that run in these offices. The opening or closing of an office will clearly change the number of service requests that occur. This is consistent with the lifecycle view of systems presented in Chapter 4. Events may not result in coding changes to systems, but they do result in changes in how the systems are utilized, and if IT is not in the loop on these business events, its systems are at greater risk of suffering a failure as a result. Ultimately, it is the responsibility of the service owner to ensure that the relationships with service consumers are healthy. Regular communication should be established with service consumers, and part of that communication should be a review of the usage metrics collected, as well as a review of any upcoming changes or business events. Likewise, a service consumer should maintain their own view of service usage, to ensure that both parties are seeing the interaction in the same way.

Defining Service Provider Baselines

In the case of service providers, baselines are established through formal performance testing. Prior to being promoted to production, testing should be performed to determine the following:

- The average response time for typical service requests. This should include an appropriate sampling of message sizes that are typical for the service usage. For example, if the message size can vary from 1KB to 1MB, both of the extremes should be tested, as well as some values in the middle.

- The CPU load for typical service requests. This may only be measurable when a sustained load is applied, rather than trying to determine the load associated with a single request.

- The memory utilization for typical service requests. Likewise, this may only be measurable when a sustained load is applied, rather than trying to determine the load associated with a single request.

- The request rate at which point some performance degradation can be detected, either in the form of increased response time, 100% CPU utilization, or 100% memory utilization.

- The request rate at which point performance becomes unacceptable, either due to sufficiently large response times or server crashes.

- Verification that no memory leaks exist when the service is placed under a sustained load for an extended period of time, simulating the system running for several weeks or months in production.

- An understanding of the scalability of the system based upon increases in the physical infrastructure allocated to the service, be it additional physical servers, CPUs or cores within existing servers, or additional memory. It is important that the service team define the scalability model.

- The impact of other service processing that may exist on the same infrastructure. While clean room testing that limits utilization to just the service in question is necessary, so is testing that simulates the production environment. A sustained background load of typical traffic for other services that share the same infrastructure should be applied.

It is critical to execute this testing in an environment as similar to production as possible. While many organizations cannot afford to have a duplicate of the production environment, at a minimum, the environment must provide performance characteristics than can be extrapolated to the production environment. For example, if the production environment contains four servers, each with two dual-core CPUs, testing on a single server that contains the same two dual-core CPUs should yield about a quarter of the capacity of production. If the testing environment instead contains a single server with a single-core CPU with less processing power, or if the testing environment leverages virtualization technology, the results may not be as easy to extrapolate to the production configuration, if even at all. Due to these challenges, it is important that service providers follow the same technique as service consumers. Baselines must be re-assessed once the service has been in production for a suitable amount of time in order to understand what normal behavior is.

These baselines are particularly important when capacity planning is taken into consideration. Many organizations have separate capacity planning teams whose job is to manage the physical infrastructure and how it is allocated to solutions. It is unlikely that an individual service will have its own dedicated infrastructure; rather, it likely shares those resources with other services. As a result, the capacity planning team must understand the resource demands of each individual service, as well as the baseline load from each consumer. As new consumers and services are preparing to go live, the capacity planning team must examine their expected resource requirements and scale the environment as needed.

Managing Run-time Usage

Once baselines have been established, the run-time infrastructure can now be properly leveraged to enforce the policies. Remember that Advasco had two policies:

- Consumers must be notified when service usage exceeds a threshold where continued usage at that rate can impact the availability to other consumers. (Advasco used email for notification, but other means such as a phone call or pages are appropriate. The exact mechanism should be negotiated with each consumer.)
- Service requests from a particular consumer must be rejected when the usage rate from that consumer exceeds a threshold, jeopardizing the stability of the service and its availability to other consumers.

Capacity planning should factor in both the baseline resource utilization of the service provider and the expected usage by the known consumers. The baseline resource utilization yields the scalable unit of capacity. From there, it is simply a manner of determining how much capacity is needed based upon the expected request load from each consumer (peaks, not average), plus an appropriate amount of overhead. Once the capacity has been set the thresholds for notification and throttling can also be set. Clearly, the best behavior is if no notification or throttling ever happens, but at the same time, the availability of the infrastructure cannot be sacrificed. The intent of the thresholds is to handle unexpected behavior.

A service intermediary or gateway such as an ESB or XML appliance is the appropriate place to enforce these policies. By the time requests get to the actual service endpoint, it is typically too late to prevent the requests from impacting the system. An intermediary typically sees a request for a few milliseconds at most, while the service endpoint may spend significantly more, whether tens or hundreds of milliseconds. Furthermore, a change to the thresholds is simply a matter of changing a policy versus redeploying code.

One challenge associated with monitoring service usage, especially in high throughput environments, is dealing with horizontally scalable infrastructure. That is, infrastructure where capacity is added by increasing another server, device, or process, rather than by expanding the resources available to existing servers, devices, or processes. For example, a typical ESB is a software system. In order to add capacity, a new instance of the software system must be installed on another server. In the case of an appliance, a new physical device is installed.

As soon as a second software instance or appliance is added to the environment, there is a challenge with visibility. The true request load is actually the cumulative load of all intermediaries processing requests for a given service. However, the problem is that these devices or software instances typically only have visibility to the requests each device or instance processes. This is normally addressed by enforcing policy at the metrics aggregation point, typically the management console, rather than on the software instance or device itself. Metrics are pushed out from the intermediaries to the central console. The central console aggregates the metrics, applies any thresholds, and then updates the behavior of the individual intermediaries accordingly.

There may also be challenges associated with load distribution. Thresholds may be established based upon the total capacity, but that may assume an equal distribution of requests across both intermediaries and service endpoints. In reality, it is easily possible to configure an intermediary in a way such that when the aggregate of all service requests are examined, there is an equal load distribution, but for a specific service, the requests may not be evenly distributed. This must be factored in when thresholds are set. If thresholds are set too high, an unequal distribution of load could result in a system failure even though a threshold was never reached.

Detecting Potential Problems

The final desired behavior for Advasco was detecting problems before consumers report them. While the two levels of thresholds provide some comfort that warnings will be issued when behavior gets outside of the norm, this approach is still very reactionary. A threshold has been reached, notification happens, and corrective action must be taken as soon as possible.

Synthetic Transactions

A common approach that is used today to detect problems before they are reported is to leverage synthetic transactions. That is, requests are pushed through the systems in question, but they typically leverage dummy data that can be easily removed from production databases or focus on read-only operations. This is a common approach for web applications, especially ones that face the public Internet.

A company may leverage an external testing service that relies on testing points in various geographic locations, so that the support desk can know whether there are regions of their audience that are experiencing connectivity problems outside of their control. This is an important point for Internet-facing applications, since the audience may include many individuals that are not technology savvy. They may not know how to recognize a problem with their service provider versus a problem with the website they are trying to visit.

Even for intranet-based applications, synthetic transactions can add significant value. Many intranet applications are dealing with a much smaller user base, and many have very sporadic periods of usage. If a problem arises during a lull in usage, it could go undetected for quite some time. The use of regularly scheduled synthetic transactions ensures that some traffic will be flowing through the system throughout the day, and that the worst-case scenario for detection will be the time in between each scheduled transaction.

The use of synthetic transactions can certainly be extended to SOA, although the full set of synthetic transactions in use by the company must be carefully managed. For example, if a web application currently has synthetic transactions hitting it every five minutes, it is certainly possible that the services it depends on are being exercised as part of those transactions. If a separate set of synthetic transactions is created strictly for testing services, the services are now being tested twice—once as part of a consuming application and once on their own. While a service provider should never rely on consumer testing for regular health checks, we also don't want an excessive amount of redundant traffic.

Predictive Analysis

The use of synthetic transactions works very well for environments where the load on a service is sporadic, but it still is a very reactionary approach. Synthetic transactions detect problems that already exist; it's just hoped that they allow you to find out about them before an irate user or partner calls.

The state that is most desired is where we can recognize patterns and trends in the environment that are likely to lead to a problem. Corrective action can then be taken to fix the situation prior to any problem ever occurring. The multi-tiered thresholds provide some comfort, but that approach is geared toward a short-term trend, such as the number of requests in a five minute interval, or at most a sixty minute interval. They don't provide benefit in examining the long-term trends. Suppose Advasco's Claims division issued a mandate that claims checks would only be submitted by direct deposit, and told all of their agents that their clients' accounts would need to have bank account information added within three months. While there are no new applications involved, a likely scenario is that the back-end service that updates the associated client records would begin to see an increase in traffic. As with any mandate with a deadline, the closer we get to the deadline, the greater the load the service will see. We now have a business condition that changed the pattern of service utilization. Unless the historical trends are being watched, these situations will go unnoticed, just as they did for Advasco. The consumer that had the bug did not start flooding the system with requests one day, rather the number of requests increased a little bit each day, until the impact became noticeable to consumers.

There are many tools that are available for analyzing historical data, whether it is a full-blown business intelligence system, or some of the specialized management tools in the SOA space. Tools, however, can only make processes more efficient. If the desired behavior is to reduce the number of client-reported problems, the appropriate policy is to look at the metrics collected on an appropriate basis, typically at least once per business day. It is the responsibility of the service manager to strive to understand the data, and have full confidence in explaining all anomalies. Historic trends are very important to understand when something is an anomaly versus the normal variation in usage from day to day. If a service has an average response time of 60ms one week, and two weeks later it has an average response time of 80ms, this behavior must be explained; even if both cases never resulted in any errors. While 20ms may not be perceptible by the consumer, it still represents a 33% increase in response time, and this type of variation must be explained. Just as an architecture review is meant to prevent a project from proceeding down a path of poor architectural decisions, the governance processes associated with the run-time environment must strive to catch things before they become a problem. Education and prevention is a more effective long-term strategy than detection, although all three will always be necessary.

Service Management Technologies

Service management, also marketed as run-time SOA Governance tools, are another area where the vendors have tools that can assist in the governance processes. Remember that no tool will give you governance; however, tooling can make your governance processes more efficient.

In Chapter 4, there were three classes of products introduced that can play a role in policy-driven infrastructure:

- Enterprise Services Buses
- XML Appliances
- Service Management Platforms

While at first glance one would think that service management platforms would be the natural choice for providing service management capabilities, the decision is not so easy. If we use a Venn diagram to illustrate the capabilities associated with these three domains, it looks like this:

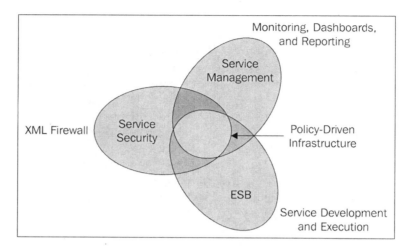

In the center is the sweet spot for policy-driven infrastructure. This includes aspects of service mediation, which is the domain of the ESB; service management, which is the domain of the service management platforms; and service security, which is the domain of the XML appliances. At the extremes of each area are capabilities that can only be found on products within those domains. In the domain of service mediation, most ESBs can also act as a service development and execution platform. Very few, if any, XML appliances or service management platforms can be used as a tool for building new services. In the domain of service management, the most sophisticated monitoring, dashboards, and reporting are only available with the service management platforms. In the domain of service security, it is typically only the XML appliances that provide sophisticated XML firewall capabilities. Therefore, when choosing infrastructure to assist in the space of run-time governance, one must look at the requirements in all of the domains, and decide whether one product can cover all of your needs or if a combination of products is the best scenario.

Within the service management space, one must also consider the domain of traditional systems management technology. Much of what was described in the Advasco example is standards systems management guidance, just applied to the domain of services. One can certainly argue that run-time governance is not exclusive to SOA, but it is true that the establishment of new boundaries and components in the form of services increases the need for effective run-time governance.

Traditional systems management technology tends to fall into the category of passive monitoring. Passive monitoring means that some monitor, be it an agent, a tap, or probe, collects the metrics. It optionally performs some analysis or posts an event, but always makes the metrics available to a centralized reporting console and dashboard. These monitors are considered passive because they have no influence on the flow of requests through the run-time infrastructure. In contrast, all of the major players in the service management platform space practice active monitoring. Their agents or gateways have the ability to not just collect metrics, but also to intercept requests and apply policy. In other words, their products contain a feedback loop between the metric collection and the policy enforcement. In order to determine that a consumer is exceeding a threshold for the number of requests allowed, incoming requests must be monitored. The current request rate over some pre-configured interval is then updated, and fed back into the policy enforcement infrastructure. On the next request, the infrastructure stops it in its tracks, checks the current request rate, and only allows the request to pass if the threshold for throttling has not been reached.

Regardless of the particular technology chosen for service management capabilities, whether the more primitive capabilities of an XML appliance or ESB, an extension of existing enterprise systems management technology, or a dedicated services management platform, you should strive to leverage an open system. The feedback loop described earlier can be shown like this:

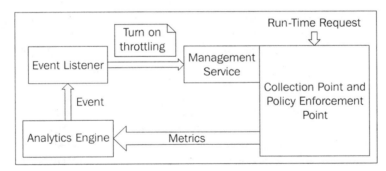

The policy enforcement point, which is also the metrics collection point, collects metrics and sends them to some analytics engine. The analytics engine can determine if a threshold has been reached, and fire off an event. This same technique also applies to other areas, such as exception management. Rather than a threshold on number of requests, there may also be threshold on the number of failed requests that need to trigger action. The same analytics engine can perform analysis on the metrics and issue events based upon the policies governing the interaction.

A listener will receive the event and issue a service invocation via a management service at the collection point to tell it to start throttling requests for a particular consumer, or whatever action is appropriate. While most traditional systems management products provide the metric collection and the analytics engine, they lack the listener with direct integration into the management services of the enforcement point. However, if the enterprise systems management can publish events in a standard form, it is entirely possible that a BPM engine or a simple JMS listener can be leveraged to listen for the event and then invoke the management services of the enforcement point to make the change, provided the enforcement point exposes such a service. As long as the monitoring and analytics technology has the capability to publish events that can be consumed outside of its boundaries, and the enforcement point is exposing its management capabilities as services, this process can be completely automated, just as it is done with a services management platform. In the same vein, if a services management platform is leveraged, while it may provide these feedback loops implicitly, it may not allow its own analytics engine to publish events outside of its boundary, or it may not expose its management capabilities via service interfaces. This leads to a closed system, which limits its long-term value in the enterprise.

Summary

This chapter focused on run-time SOA governance. While this topic was briefly touched upon in Chapter 4 with regards to versioning, this chapter filled in the remaining details. As governance is about people, policies, and processes put in place to achieve a desired behavior, run-time SOA governance is about the people, policies, and processes put in place to ensure the desired behavior of the systems involved at run-time.

The service consumer must specify an expected load that their system will place on the service provider, while the service provider must specify the resource consumption associated with an invocation of the service. This establishes the baseline behavior from which policies can be created that establish monitoring thresholds and associated activities when those thresholds are breached, whether it be notifications or throttling/rejection of requests.

Historical observations are critical for the proper management of the system; simply relying on infrastructure that provides alerts when a pre-determined threshold is reached or a heartbeat fails is not sufficient. By constantly observing the run-time behavior of the system, trends can be noticed, insights can be gained, and the service can be continually improved.

Infrastructure that can assist in this effort falls into the same three categories mentioned in Chapter 4: ESB technology, XML Appliances, and Service Management Platforms. Each technology domain has its strengths and weaknesses, but there is a significant amount of overlap across them. The needs of your organization will dictate whether you need a single product from one domain, or two or more products from multiple domains to meet your needs. The key is in ensuring that the products chosen have an open, extensible architecture.

7
SOA Success

So what does SOA success look like? What happens when your governance efforts are successful in changing the behavior of the organization? This chapter will give you a picture of what outcomes can arise by describing Advasco five years from the time they initiated their efforts. Change does not happen overnight, and the change associated with SOA adoption must be viewed as a long-term commitment.

Celebrating Success

Spencer's day began almost like every other day. Traffic was kind to him this morning, and he arrived a few minutes earlier than normal. He was walking in from the parking garage when he ran into Elena.

"How are you this morning, Spencer?" she asked.

"I'm doing well. The traffic over the bridge was a lot better than normal, so that always helps to start the day off right," he replied.

"The traffic was pretty good for me, as well. It's been a while since that happened!"

"Hey, do you know what Andrea is going to talk about at the Town Hall today? Things have been going so well, I'm curious what she's going to say! In years past, she's always had to pass along the latest complaint from outside of IT and rally us to do something about it, but I haven't heard any rumblings at all. My contacts outside of IT can't stop talking about the good job we're doing for a change."

"I'm as much in the dark as you are with this one, Spencer," she replied. "While she's consulted me prior to Town Halls before, she's been silent about this one."

"Oh well, I guess we'll all find out soon enough. Well, hopefully the demeanor outside of IT is an accurate indicator, and there will be nothing but good news at the meeting."

"I think you can be pretty confident about that. If there were any chance the news was going to be bad, I'd be aware of it. I've got a few things I need to take care of this morning, so I'll see you at the meeting."

"Have a great day, Elena, I'll see you at ten."

"Shortly before ten o'clock, Spencer stepped into the auditorium and spotted the rest of the SOA Center of Excellence, along with Elena, Maria, and some of the other key people who had been involved in Advasco's SOA efforts. They were all chatting idly waiting for the meeting to begin. Spencer sat down next to Maria and asked her, "Do you have any idea what Andrea is going to talk about?"

"No, I don't. I've been trying to figure it out as well! You'd think we were going to an Apple announcement with the secrecy around this meeting," she replied.

"I think we're about to find out, here comes Andrea," he said.

Andrea walked into the auditorium with a smile on her face. Of course, she had good reason to smile, and was excited about having the opportunity to share it with the rest of IT.

"I want to thank all of you for taking the time out of your schedules for another Town Hall. From what I gather, there's a lot of speculation going around on what I'm going to talk about today. Given my track record with these Town Halls, you're used to me talking about something that needs to be improved. Well today, we're not going to do that. Instead, I'm going to focus on our success — success with SOA."

"Five years ago to the day we began our SOA efforts. At that time, Advasco was taking a beating. Our customer satisfaction rating was one of the lowest in the industry, and our executive team decided we needed to do something about it. Our analysis of the problem indicated that one of the biggest problems we had was the disparate customer systems for our different financial products."

"Elena, our Chief Architect, assigned Spencer to assist in that effort, knowing that he had an interest in service-oriented architecture. That event kicked off our SOA efforts. I don't know if all of you realize just how far we've come, but I wanted to take some time to put it all in perspective for all of you."

"Five years ago Advasco's IT department consisted of many silos, each with their own systems that could be best described as 'forced integration'. That is, our systems only talked to each other when we were absolutely forced to do so. We struggled with delivering timely solutions. We had multiple implementations of the same functionality scattered all over IT, and not just two or three, but sometimes five or six different implementations. We lacked the necessary metrics to really understand the value that our solutions were providing to the business. It had reached the point where we were at a competitive disadvantage at least partly due to the state of our IT systems."

"Beginning with our Customer systems, we began a journey to change that. While our initial focus was limited to the auto and home insurance groups, the success of the effort eventually led us to a single view of customers across all of our lines of business, something our competitors have not been able to duplicate so far. Today, I am happy to report to you that Advasco has been named the number one company in our industry for customer satisfaction for the last year. It is thanks to the hard work of all of you, and in my opinion, the efforts that IT led in embracing SOA not just within IT, but throughout Advasco, that made it possible. So, today, we're going to do a bit of reminiscing. People often say that things are so slow to change, and when you're looking at it from one day to the next, it can seem that way. However, when we look back five years we can really see exactly how far we've come and how much we've changed."

"Our efforts to adopt SOA weren't easy by any means. In the early stages, there were more than our fair share of detractors who simply wanted to keep building systems the way we've always built systems."

Spencer looked around the room and made eye contact with Ramesh. Ramesh gave him a little smirk, knowing that his project manager had fought the move to SOA in the beginning. Ramesh was able to reverse that decision two years later and share in the success.

"Admittedly, we also had our blind supporters. I'll be the first one to confess that we were a bit too eager to bask in the glow of our initial success. I'm sure Elena and Spencer still wish that I had consulted with them a bit more before delivering my Town Hall message asking the staff to embrace SOA."

This was part of the reason that Andrea had the respect of all of the IT staff. Her insight was normally excellent, but she also wasn't afraid to admit that sometimes that insight needed to be fleshed out in a bit more detail before unveiling it to everyone. The staff respected her candor. Elena and Spencer both were pleased that Andrea called this out, since it created some unique challenges for them in trying to encourage the adoption of SOA at Advasco.

"While the staff did embrace SOA exactly as I had asked, that simply led us down a path of service silos. We had lots of services, but things didn't look any different. We had the same solutions we always had; only now they had services inside of them. In fact, we sometimes had two or three services that did the same thing. This had a risk of increasing the complexity of our IT landscape, but thankfully, we made some changes to address that."

"It began by recognizing that in order to have services that could be reused someone needed to be responsible for the delivery of the service, not just for their own needs, but for the needs of the organization."

"On hearing this, Maria remembered vividly her discussions with Jim and Beth on who would own and deliver the service for account information. Jim and Beth were seated a few rows back as well, and Jim took the advantage of the opportunity to remind Maria by saying, "Andrea, I nominate Maria for the effort!"

Everyone laughed, knowing that Maria had become one of the strongest mentors in the organization to new service managers. She had become the resident expert on how to embrace a consumer-centric philosophy within a team, and other teams that were struggling with delivery to their consumers were constantly seeking her out for advice.

"I'm sure many of you would like to have Maria managing the services in your areas. But as we learned, having one single expert is not enough. While we didn't let it go that far, relying heavily on one person typically results in that person being very overworked and at extreme risk of burning out, taking our chances for success with them. Rather, we realized that we needed to have a broader perspective and create an environment for growth and success from many people. To enable this, we created a Center of Excellence; one that I believe was instrumental to getting us to where we are today."

"The Center of Excellence began by filling in the details that I had left out in my Town Hall, and providing an answer to the question 'Why SOA?' to the organization. They then set out, acting as mentors and mediators on projects, educating and enlightening as they went along. They probably could have stopped there, and have many of their efforts considered successful for that year's review, but the team did not view that as success. Rather, they recognized that they needed to be more engaged with the projects occurring in the enterprise, rather than being exclusively focused on education and communication."

Raj and Jared both remembered those initial meetings with Spencer, when the team was feeling particularly frustrated about their ability to make an impact in the way that projects were building their solutions. Their perseverance paid off in the long run.

"They took on the burden of working with all of our projects to ensure that the teams were aware of services that existed, and that the rest of the organization found out about new services that were being created. They facilitated the ownership decisions that naturally occurred when multiple projects recognized the need for a common service. In short, this team established the initial policies that represented the desired behavior we needed in our development practices, and then made sure those policies were followed through a combination of education and active mentoring."

"This was just the first of many examples where the COE recognized that things were becoming stagnant, and that new efforts were needed to keep things moving forward. The next hurdle came when we had to make changes to one of our key services. Many of my colleagues at other companies have said to me, 'How did you do it? As soon as we had to make a change to a service, everything started to unravel.' We did it because we didn't just slap together a solution for that service. Instead, the COE recognized that things will change, and that we need to plan for change, rather than react when it happens. They introduced the concept of Service Lifecycle Management to our efforts, which represented a significant departure from the way we've traditionally done things. We all had to stop thinking in terms of projects and start thinking in terms of the delivery of capabilities."

"Several of you jumped right on this concept, and for those key services that had been created and changed, this proved to be very valuable. Unfortunately, we still hadn't reached the point where we wanted to be. From my perspective, there still seemed to be quite a bit of scrambling that occurred at the beginning of projects in trying to determine the services necessary for the solution. Even worse, the majority of our services were still only appropriate for the project in which they were created. Finally, I saw a number of services that in subsequent releases had capability additions or modifications that made me wonder, 'How did we miss that with the original version?'

My initial thoughts were to turn to the COE, but instead, I asked our chief architect, Elena, to gather up some of the best service managers we had and discuss this problem. In their analysis, the team recognized that all policies and processes defined by the COE had been followed. Rather than continue to look for something that had been performed incorrectly, the team decided to look for ways that things could be changed."

"I'm sure many, if not all of you, have heard the definition of insanity attributed to Albert Einstein. He said, 'The definition of insanity is doing the same thing over and over again and expecting different results.' This is a very important point that all of us need to remember. If we're not achieving the results we hope for, simply stating that we're not achieving those results and then going back to our cubicles and doing the same work we were doing will not change anything. When I came up here years ago and simply told all of you to embrace SOA, did that change the outcome? Yes, we did get services, but they were a drop-in replacement for something else. So, in reality, nothing did change. Now, when we were confronted with the question of how to ensure that the 'right' services get built, simply telling our analysts to work harder was not going to cut it."

"The team determined that a change was needed in the contextual information available to the project teams. Without proper context, the team was going to continue to make decisions based upon the scope associated with that project. Even when services were broken out of those projects, the initial context was still rooted there. I see that a few of you may not quite grasp this, so let me try to give you a comparison point. When you go to the grocery store, do you buy just the food you need for the next meal, or do you buy the food you need for the entire week? If you only knew about your next meal, you'd only buy the food you needed for that meal. Suppose the recipe included milk, and suppose you went to your neighbors and asked them if they needed milk too. They might, and you might buy enough for them. What's the problem here? Did you ask them if they needed anything else from the store? Did you check your planned meals for the rest of the week and see if you needed more of anything, or other items that you hadn't thought of? The whole part of actions was influenced by the initial context of your next meal and the fact that it needed milk. This, unfortunately, is how we executed our projects."

"The fundamental change that was needed was to provide more context going into these efforts. If you had your meals planned out for the entire week, your grocery shopping would probably be much more efficient over the course of the week, wouldn't it? Such was the case for us. We needed to provide better context before starting our projects to enable us to be more efficient in their delivery."

"To do this, we engaged a local consulting firm to assist us in developing our business architecture. The artifacts from this effort broke down the capabilities of our businesses into services in increasing detail, enabling us to see where opportunities for reuse existed, and where, given our current business model, opportunities for reuse should not be pursued. It was far easier to determine the areas of immediate need and demand as a result. The best part of this was that the decision to pursue a business architecture was not made by IT leadership; rather Advasco leadership, including my counterparts, made it. Through our efforts in embracing SOA and demonstrating the optimizations that we had made, it was clear that changes were needed outside of IT to continue our progress. We took a service-oriented view of the entire business, not just IT, which naturally made our SOA efforts much more aligned with our overall corporate goals, causing more significant change."

"No longer were we asked to deliver particular projects, rather our efforts began to split into service development efforts associated with the business service domains identified in our business architecture, and clear consumption domains that represented the systems that our users typically interact with directly. From this point on, my executive counterparts have been as big of a proponent of SOA as we have."

"That commitment became very important when we ran into some challenges with our first services exposed to our external partners. I'm sure that most of us gathered here know that when you're inside your own house, it's far easier to get away with less than perfect behavior. When I take my kids to someone else's house, however, I always tell them, 'I want you to be on your best behavior.' Unfortunately, that's not what happens each time. We had gotten away with some immature monitoring and management practices, whether by luck or just putting up with it, and I take full responsibility for not setting the bar for what was expected. It was a good learning lesson for all of us. We learned that while we still need to be monitoring our systems for failures, it is equally important, if not more important, to understand what the typical run-time behavior is, and always look into deviations from that behavior."

"So where are we today? We have hundreds of services in production. Some are strictly used by internal consumers, some are strictly used by external consumers, and some are used by both. Some have one consumer, some have many consumers, but nearly all of them are meeting our expectations on the number of consumers. Where we expected reuse, we're getting it, and in other areas, where we've built services for reasons other than reuse, such as reducing the time to respond to regulatory changes, we're seeing those results."

"More dramatic is the change that has occurred within the organization, both within IT and outside of IT. Previously IT was very closely aligned to specific business areas and the applications within them. Today, both the non-IT organizations and the IT organization are aligned along services and service consumers. The business architecture we have developed clearly indicates those areas where reuse and standardization has the most value, and the areas where specialization and customization has the most value. The organizational structure follows this, and as a result, we are widely considered to have the best resource utilization in the industry. Rather than being the ones who respond to the change occurring in our industry, we are now the ones driving the change in the industry, and our stock price shows it. We have made a fundamental change in the way we utilize IT, one that has put us years ahead of our competition. This change is not rooted in the particular technologies that we have chosen to use, but rather in the way that we behave, from how we define the IT efforts we invest in, to the way we manage those solutions when they are in production. Ask any expert on business improvement, and they will tell you the hardest thing to change is corporate culture and behavior. Well, we've done it, and all of you should be commended for it."

"In recognition of this feat, I am pleased to pass along an announcement from our board of directors and CEO. First, in recognition of the hard work and time that has been spent in achieving this goal, Advasco is returning some of that time to you and your families. The four days between Christmas and New Years Day will be paid company holidays this year. For those of you that are in operational positions that require that you work these days, you will be given four additional holidays to use at other times in the year. Second, the company will be issuing a stock grant of 100 shares to all employees with at least six months of service as of today. This is both a recognition of what we've achieved, as well as an incentive for everyone to keep up the hard work, as these shares will be even more valuable five years from now as long as we strive to always be changing our behavior in ways that will improve our results. Our SOA efforts are successful, but they are not over. Keep up the good work!"

Changing Behavior

If this narrative has not made it clear, the key to success with SOA lies not with the technologies you choose, but the changes in behavior you are able to make. Changing behavior is one of the most difficult things an individual can do, and is even harder for an organization. It is an effort that will not happen in days, weeks, or months, but over years. Milestones must be established to guide the path along the way, and the journey is never over.

One only needs to look at the struggles many people have with weight loss to understand the difficulty in changing behavior. My desired goal may be to lose twenty pounds, and there are many ways of achieving that goal. I can make many short-term decisions to achieve that goal, such as skipping meals, but if my behavior does not change, those twenty pounds will quickly return, and possibly even more.

Such is the same with SOA. As shown in the Advasco example, an organization can quickly build services, but this may not yield any reduction in the cost of IT solutions, the speed in which they are delivered, the responsiveness of IT to changing business demand, or any of the other lofty goals frequently associated with SOA. A specialized program can be created around a specific change occurring, much like what occurred in the late 1990's when companies had to build an Internet presence. Did the companies get a website up and running? Absolutely! Did those websites make dramatic changes to those businesses? In a few cases, yes, but in the majority of cases, they did not. If anything, in many cases it simply made things more confusing and more complex, because it was not clear how those Web presences integrated into the company's operating model. Many companies built their website, and then went right back to the old way of doing things, only now with the maintenance costs of an under-utilized Web presence weighing them down.

The Inherent Risk of Governance

If you were to go into ten different IT departments and ask them for their thoughts on governance, chances are that at least nine of ten, if not all ten, would have a negative reaction. To many, governance creates visions of a review board or police force that is completely disconnected with reality, and that simply gets in the way and does more to keep work from getting done than actually improving things.

To counter this prevailing opinion, one must redefine governance. This book consistently uses the definition of the people, policies, and processes that an organization employs to ensure a desired behavior. When establishing governance in an organization, the focus, first and foremost, needs to be on the behavior. All too often, the focus is placed on the people, policies, and processes, without ever having communicated the desired behavior. If that behavior is not clear, then all remaining activities will be questioned. For a particular problem, is it possible that a single team of developers building it from end-to-end can get it done faster? Yes. Is getting the project completed as quickly as possible the desired behavior? Not necessarily. Schedule is certainly an important factor, and for people working on that project, including the project manager, that may be the subject that comes up most frequently. If the staff is not educated on the other important desired behaviors that also impact long-term decisions, they cannot be expected to change their behavior without strong resistance.

In Andrea's speech to IT, never once did she mention the word "governance," but the word "change" was used throughout. At the end of her talk, she even emphasized that it wasn't a change in technology that had led to their success, it was the changes in behavior they made. If there is a message that needs to be communicated, it is not that an organization needs SOA governance; rather it is that an organization needs to change their behavior. Furthermore, in order for continued success, the organization must embrace change, and always strive to be improving. Advasco never settled for some of the short-term success they had achieved throughout their efforts. Rather, when initial success was achieved, the next step was to look for more success, always building upon the work that had been done. It is not surprising that industry observers have frequently recognized that the companies that have the greatest need are often the ones that never achieve the benefits, yet the companies that are already ahead of the pack and succeeding tend to adopt new approaches like SOA far more easily, even though the relative benefits for them are likely less. This is because the corporate culture of the more successful companies is one of continued improvement, always looking for ways to improve, rather than being resistant to anything other than the status quo, despite the apparent need.

For this reason, it is important to first recognize where your company is today, and determine what the desired behavior is. If it's not a significant change from where you currently are, a change to the corporate culture that introduces rigid review processes, Centers of Excellence and more, could do more harm than good. For an organization whose current behavior is far removed from the desired behavior, a more abrupt change may be the only thing that will get them there. The one golden rule when it comes to governance is that the most successful approach is when you can make compliance the path of least resistance. The right combination of education, automation, structure, and enforcement must be leveraged to make that happen.

Changing Governance Over Time

Finally, your approach to governance must evolve and change over time. Advasco continually was faced with new situations that required new people, policies, and processes, and that was solely based on the changing questions of building services the "right" way, building the "right" services, and ensuring the run-time environment behaved properly. The examples didn't cover other possible changes such as growth in the company, mergers and acquisitions, or regulatory changes from outside the organization.

Back at the beginning of the book, the topic of governance was introduced using typical municipal governance. This is a good example for understanding the impact of changes in the environment. What is the impact on a city's governance when it grows from 5,000 people to 15,000 people? It is likely that some stop signs have turned to traffic lights, and some changes to the speed limit on certain roads have been made. It is also likely that the city has added to its police force. However, these are the simple ones. The bigger challenge is heavily dependent on the 10,000 people that were added. Is the average annual income of these people $50,000 or $500,000?

Putting this in context of a typical corporation, if a company acquires another company in a different geographical region, how will the governance effort extend to cover the efforts in that region? Simply put, they must change. It could be as simple as putting the new staff through an education curriculum, it could require adding people from that new location to the policy-making board, or it could require amending policies, since the location of development may dictate whether redundant services are allowed or not.

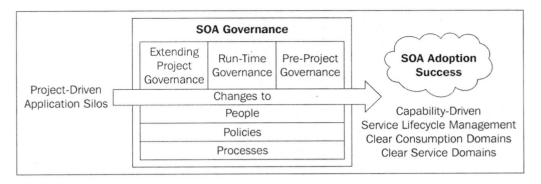

Summary

Adopting SOA does not consist of one or two projects or one large program. Rather, it is an effort that will likely take several years. In reality there is no "completed" state, just as there is no completed state associated with application development. There were always new applications to build or existing ones that required modification. It is important to stop and take assessment of the progress that has been made at regular intervals, but more importantly, to ensure that the change in behavior that was desired is occurring. Establishing governance to guide behavior is not a simple task, and when the environment changes your approach to governance needs to change with it. It may mean involving new people, establishing new policies, or changing your processes. In the end, governance is a key to changing the behavior of your organization to meet the goals desired by your SOA efforts.

8

Establishing SOA Governance at Your Organization

The adoption of SOA can represent a fundamental change in the way you deliver technology solutions. While many books have been written on the technical aspects of SOA, it is the cultural aspects that can pose the biggest challenge. An organization must learn how to break down the boundaries that have built up over time, and leverage the assets available to them in a more effective manner. SOA governance is about establishing the appropriate structure to guide an organization through this change with people, policies, and process. While it can begin as an extension to the normal project governance process to include appropriate use of service technologies like XML, SOAP, or REST, it must go beyond the core technology guidance and into changes in how development teams interact with each other across the organization, changes in how services and their consumers are managed at run-time, and changes in how an organization determines what solutions will be built in the first place.

This book has presented the story of a fictitious company, Advasco, and their experiences with SOA governance. Some of their examples may have been very relevant to your own organization, and some of them may have not. Every company is unique with its own corporate culture. A Center of Excellence may be required for success at one organization, while another organization may not need to establish that level of formality. One company may get significant benefit out of a commercial Registry/Repository product while another company may achieve the same benefits by utilizing an open-source wiki. Factors such as company size, IT structure, IT locations, business goals, and competition are some of many that play a role in determining the right approach. In all cases, if your company does not clearly articulate its desired behavior, have people responsible for establishing the policies that will elicit the behavior, have consistent policies throughout the organization, and establish processes for education, communication, measurement, and enforcement, you will struggle.

This chapter will walk through the three major components of a successful SOA governance effort: people, policies, and processes. Various areas will be covered that a company must consider when adopting SOA. Some may be areas that are not applicable; some may be areas that are very applicable. Use it as a cookbook for determining the right SOA governance approach for your organization.

People

There are many different people that can play a role in your SOA governance efforts. This section will go over the various roles and their responsibilities within SOA governance, whether it be in establishing policies, or in the processes associated with education, communication, measurement, or enforcement. It will also call out how these various roles can be organized and the various engagement models that can be utilized.

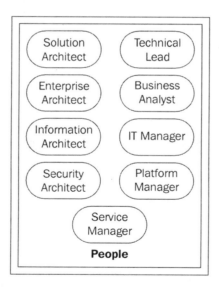

Solution Architect

The solution architect is the person responsible for the technical leadership and decisions on a project or program. Being the technical decision maker, this person is responsible for the project's compliance with the technical design-time policies. This includes both the solution's architecture, for which the person likely has direct responsibilities, as well as the solution's design, for which the person will be working with the developers and other project staff. Typically, the solution architect has a larger role in ensuring that services are built the right way. In ensuring that the right services get built, the solution architect must work closely with the lead analyst on the project.

The solution architect is also responsible for ensuring that the appropriate run-time governance policies are established. If the project delivers a service consumer, the solution architect must work with the lead analyst to determine the expected usage for all services. If the project delivers a service provider, the solution architect must determine the resource consumption associated with a service invocation.

It is important to remember that the solution architect is a role. Your organization may not have a formal job title of solution architect, but someone will play this role on each and every project.

Business Analyst

The business analyst is the counterpart to the solution architect on a project, focusing on the functional aspects of the solution. They frequently perform requirements gathering activities, create use case diagrams, and may also be responsible for business process modeling. A more senior business analyst will have a significant amount of domain knowledge and may have key relationships within the organization outside of IT.

Within the SOA governance effort, business analysts play a key role in determining the appropriate functional boundaries for services. If you are able to move beyond the boundaries of projects and pursue the development of business architecture models, as discussed in Chapter 5, business analysts may be a significant part of the effort. If your enterprise architecture organization is focused on technology architecture, an effort to establish business architecture will require the domain knowledge of your most senior business analysts.

Technical Lead/Domain Architect

The technical lead and/or application architect is typically the job title associated with individuals that act as solution architects. Frequently, however, these individuals also have domain architecture responsibilities. That is, they may have oversight over several projects within a particular domain, or a role in establishing reference architectures within a particular domain outside of the context of any particular project.

Clearly, these individuals have a role in the many of the governance policies discussed earlier in the book. If an organization chooses to establish a SOA Center of Excellence, it is very likely that the domain architects will play a significant role. The domain architecture provides context for all of the projects that are executed within that domain. This can include business process analysis or business architecture development, as discussed earlier. It may also include guidance for particular technologies that are only used within that domain, such as ERP modules.

A particular challenge for this role is that these individuals frequently come from a development background, rather than an analyst background. The differences in architecture from domain to domain are typically not in the technologies utilized, but the functional domains involved. If these individuals do not have the proper functional knowledge of their business domains, they need to work closely with the key analysts in their organizations.

Finally, the technical leads must have clear and open communication with each other. It is likely that the current organizational structure does not reflect the boundaries between service consumers and service providers, meaning that there is significant redundancy across those domains. In the early stages of SOA adoption, these domain architects must work together to provide assistance to the IT managers in determining appropriate ownership.

Enterprise Architect/Technology Architect

The enterprise architect plays a very similar role to that of the domain architect. The key difference is that enterprise architects normally deal within domains that are applicable to the entire enterprise. This tends to include all of the pure technology domains, as well as security. Recently, enterprise architecture is expanding into the business architecture space, being seen as a key to aligning IT with the rest of the company. Organizations that are embracing business architecture will likely include domain architects as part of their enterprise architecture team.

In terms of SOA governance, the enterprise architect, like the domain architect, is typically in an oversight position, rather than being an active project team member. Enterprise architects are frequently responsible for strategies, roadmaps, reference architectures, and patterns that project teams are expected to implement and utilize. Therefore, enterprise architects are clearly well-positioned to provide governance. A reference architecture or design pattern is nothing more than a collection of policies that ensure solutions are built the appropriate way.

Enterprise architects that are more focused on technology architecture are responsible for the infrastructure strategy. Earlier in the book, a number of alternatives were presented for implementing policy-driven infrastructure. If enterprise architecture handles technology architecture, then it is their responsibility to set the direction in this space. This also includes ensuring that application teams use the infrastructure properly. This is an especially important concern in the SOA space primarily due to the emergence of the Enterprise Service Bus. No two ESBs are alike, as products marketed as an ESB come from **EAI (Enterprise Application Integration)** technology, **MOM (Message-Oriented Middleware)** technology, network appliances, and even products that are built from scratch. It is up to the enterprise architect to provide clarity on how an ESB should be utilized, if even at all. One of the questions that SOA governance must address is how to ensure that services are built the right way; clearly, the policies that ensure this behavior are the domain of the enterprise architect.

Enterprise architects that have business architecture responsibilities have an even larger role in the SOA governance efforts. The second major question is how to ensure the right services get built, and as discussed in Chapter 5, the key is business architecture and the creation of appropriate business domain models, possibly including business process models or business capability maps. The enterprise architect that is focused on business architecture has a role in performing the analysis and incorporating the business strategy into these business domain models that ultimately will be used in the project definition process to ensure the right services get built.

Information Architect

The information architect is a role that sometimes may get overlooked in SOA governance. A key challenge in adopting SOA is striving for consistent representations of information on service messages. Frequently, information architects may not be involved in this discussion because the conversation is typically between developers or solution architects. As a result, the representation of the information may be rooted in the processing models of the service consumers and service provider. This is neither good nor bad, but it does not take into account any storage model of the information, or any work that may be done by an information governance council in trying to define a canonical model or data dictionary.

In order for an organization to strive for consistency in the representation of information, it is important to include information architecture in the SOA governance efforts for service design, specifically in providing context for defining the schemas of the service messages.

Security Architect

The security architect is the role associated with ensuring that the technology solutions of the company take appropriate measures to protect its sensitive information, whether for protection of intellectual property, or for privacy protection related to the information maintained by the company. It is very likely that security architects are already involved with governance, whether it is part of broad IT governance related to Sarbanes-Oxley, or more exclusively focused on security policies.

One key area of focus for the security architect with regards to SOA governance is the role of identity in service interactions. Run-time governance techniques, such as traffic shaping/request throttling, are completely dependent on having identity of the consumer. As the degree of interactions between services increases, determining exactly what identity should be passed through these interactions is a challenge, and one that will require the guidance of your security architects.

IT Manager

The role of the typical IT manager is to manage personnel, manage work, and manage budget. This role is absolutely critical to the success of the SOA, because the changes that can be achieved have the most impact on IT management. Developers will still be writing code, but managers will have their entire world changed. IT managers that previously had complete control over their applications now may be dependent on other IT managers, or have other IT managers dependent on them. While most organizations are already dealing with this when it comes to infrastructure dependencies, many are not dealing with application-to-application dependencies.

If we look significantly forward, a successful SOA adoption can lead to significant organizational changes. IT managers may be reluctant to embrace this change as they may feel that their power is being taken away from them. Upper management tends to remain stable, and the people working in the trenches will still be doing analysis, project management, or development, but middle management has no such guarantees.

In order to mitigate this risk, it is important that IT management, specifically the middle managers, take an active role in the early decisions around service ownership.

Service Manager/Owner

The service manager, also known as the service owner, is a new role to most organizations, although if your organization has adopted ITIL and ITSM, you may have some familiarity with the concepts, but focused on services provided by IT operations. The service manager is the person responsible for managing the relationships with service consumers, scheduling and executing the upcoming releases of the service, and establishing relationships and service contracts with new consumers.

The service manager plays a key role in ensuring proper run-time governance is in place. Ultimately, the service manager, as the name suggests, is responsible for the service that is provided to the consumers, and the last thing needed is to have a service outage. The service manager must ensure that all details of the service contract have been established and that the infrastructure has been properly configured to enforce the policies within the service contract.

Initially, service managers may come from IT, but it is entirely possible that service managers may also be placed outside of IT, especially where services are exposed to external partners.

Platform Manager

The platform manager is responsible for the technology platform where services (and consumers, for internal consumers) are hosted. For most organizations that do not have the role of service manager defined, it falls to the operations team, whether an individual engineer or team or their associated manager to ensure that no outages occur in production.

Even when an organization does have a service manager role, the platform manager is still responsible for the underlying platforms, effectively providing a hosting service for the solutions that are deployed on them, whether those solutions represent service consumers or service providers. An individual service manager is primarily concerned about their service, and may not be watching the entire platform. Furthermore, for a service that involves several systems in its implementation, multiple platform managers may be involved, while the service manager is still responsible for the end-to-end performance of the entire service implementation across all systems, as illustrated by the following diagram:

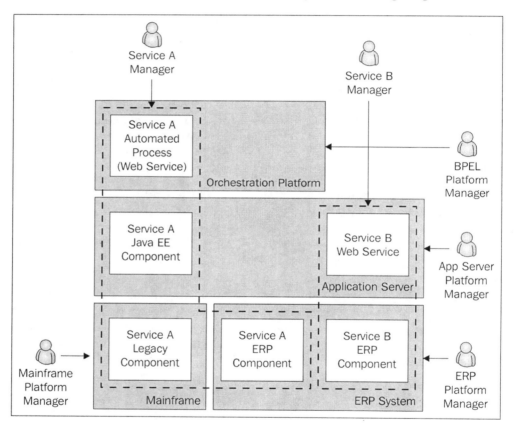

In this diagram, Service A is comprised of components that run on an orchestration platform (BPEL engine), an application server, a mainframe, and an ERP system. The manager for Service A must be concerned with the end-to-end performance across the platforms. Service B is comprised of a Web Service hosted on the application server platform and an ERP component. The manager for Service B is concerned with these two components. In contrast, each of these platforms has a platform manager that is concerned with the overall performance of the platform and each component running on it. The manager of the application server platform is concerned about the performance and capacity of the application server platform and must watch the performance of the Java EE component of Service A, and the web service of Service B, but is otherwise unconcerned about the remaining components that constitute Service A and Service B.

The platform manager is involved with establishing the entry criteria in order for a component to be deployed on a platform in a production environment. For example, if it is determined that a service did not use the appropriate instrumentation framework to allow for operational monitoring, it should not be allowed to go into production, since it can put the entire platform at risk.

Other Stakeholders

Besides the individuals already mentioned, there are other stakeholders that will play a role in your SOA governance efforts. While the majority of the technical governance issues are covered by the existing roles that have been identified, there are additional roles that may be involved with the non-technical governance. These individuals are likely already involved with your normal IT governance efforts, such as members of review boards that approve capital expenditures and project requests. Rather than forming additional committees designed to be involved in the governance process, it is better to ensure that the desired behaviors and goals for SOA are factored into the existing governance process.

Organizing Your People

There are many different organizational approaches that can be leveraged for your SOA governance efforts. SOA adoption is an enterprise initiative, however, which creates a challenge. Of the roles mentioned, only the Enterprise Architect, the Information Architect, and the Security Architect normally operate at the enterprise level. The remaining roles are either focused on project activities, on segments of technology, or on segments of the business. At the same time, many Enterprise Architectures are heavily focused on the underlying technology platforms, and may not have the appropriate functional knowledge to contribute to defining the functional boundaries associated with SOA adoption. As was shown in the Advasco story, both the technology architecture and the functional architecture are key aspects of SOA. Information architects are similar to enterprise architects in that they have broad visibility, but in a narrow area; in this case, the data systems of the enterprise. A similar story holds true for security architects.

Given the plethora of roles available, but the lack of the right role, it is important that the organization determine an approach to ensuring a successful adoption of SOA. There are a variety of different techniques that can be used.

Enterprise Architecture Driven

In this approach, the responsibility for SOA adoption lies solely within the enterprise architecture team. This can be a very good fit for many of the project governance concerns, and even some of the run-time governance concerns, since Enterprise Architecture is frequently tasked with driving strategic technologies into the enterprise. If your Enterprise Architecture team is also responsible for business architecture, then it is in an even stronger position, as it can also handle many of the pre-project governance concerns. The risk, however, is that technology is just a small part of SOA. The greater challenge is the cultural changes both in the way projects are defined and the way they are built. This can be a much more difficult task for Enterprise Architecture, since they are not normally in the management hierarchy with the people who will be most impacted by SOA adoption.

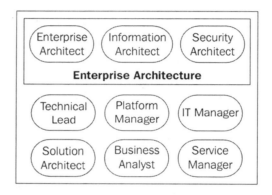

Two key relationships that can be a good litmus test before embracing an Enterprise Architecture driven SOA effort is the relationship with key IT managers, including the ability to influence organizational issues, and the relationship with key business leaders, especially those responsible for business strategy and architecture. If the Enterprise Architecture team is responsible for business architecture, chances are even better that they can drive the effort.

Another factor is the current role of Enterprise Architecture in the educational and governance processes that already exist in the enterprise. If the organization is used to taking direction and learning from Enterprise Architecture, this is a good thing. If the enterprise architects already play a role in the governance process for software development, whether through formal reviews or through less formal project engagements, again, it is not a big stretch to have them include enforcement of some of the SOA policies in their existing activities.

One risk associated with the Enterprise Architecture driven approach is the number of resources that can be dedicated to the effort. While one or more members of the EA group may be dedicated (or partially dedicated) to the effort, they need support from members of other organizations to participate in the effort. Another risk is in the area of run-time governance. An enterprise architect is normally not involved with the run-time management of production solutions. As a result, they are not as well-positioned to provide guidance on the right way to manage the services. Given the strong technology backgrounds of many enterprise architects, however, they usually have excellent relationships with the operational staff that allows for appropriate influence.

Center of Excellence/Competency Center

In this approach, the responsibility for SOA adoption is given to a cross-functional team of people. This has advantages, since it can draw from all areas of the organization and can include as many of the roles associated with SOA governance as desired. There are two factors that can have a large influence in the success of a Center of Excellence: the composition of the team and the engagement model with the organization.

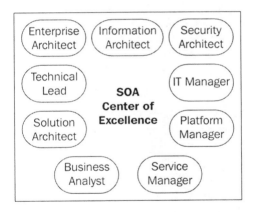

The composition of the team is the first decision that must be made by the organization. As with any virtual team, a common mistake is to choose people who have time to participate rather than choosing people who should be participating. Just as with the Enterprise Architecture driven approach, it is important that the people chosen for the Center of Excellence have the ability to influence the rest of the organization. Choose people that will struggle trying to influence others, and there's a good chance that the entire SOA effort will struggle as well.

The second factor is the engagement model with the rest of the organization. While a permanent organization like Enterprise Architecture may already have a defined engagement model with projects, a new virtual team does not. There are many nuances to the Center of Excellence that must be examined. First, what is the team's purpose? Is it to communicate a message about SOA and educate the rest of the organization? If this is the only focus, there is a risk that the effort will become disconnected from the projects that are realizing the organization's SOA. If the Center of Excellence tries to remain connected by participating on projects, how will that occur? At a minimum, the Center of Excellence can act as a reviewer for projects. A second option is to act as a staffing center for the projects. This is a common approach for Competency Centers, where a goal of the group is to train other staff members by working alongside them. This works well for the more technical areas of SOA, such as teaching staff how to work with XML or Web Services, but it may not be as practical for the non-technical aspects. A third approach is to act as an outsourcing center for service development. This approach has benefits in that the development of key services can be separated from the projects that identified the need, allowing them to be developed in a way that benefits a broader audience. The inherent risk with this approach is that the Center of Excellence may not have the domain knowledge of the functional areas necessary to develop the services properly. Once again, it is likely that a team can be formed with the necessary technical skills, but it is far more difficult to staff a team with the necessary functional knowledge. Furthermore, it is not possible for a small, centralized team to own all services in the organization. Eventually, this approach will not scale. Your goal must be to establish service development and service integration as a standard capability of the entire organization, not just one team.

A successful approach for a Center of Excellence is to initially focus heavily on communication and education, along with providing some amount of resources that assist in staffing initial projects. Rather than have work outsourced to them, they provide staff to projects that can train other people, ensure compliance of the SOA governance policies within those projects, and also bring back feedback to the Center of Excellence on policies that encountered resistance or were problematic to implement. Over time, the need to be a staffing center will go away, but the need for SOA governance will not. The Center of Excellence must still be a source of policies, an arbitrator when policies are conflicting or confusing, a source of consulting for decision guidance, continued education and communication on the SOA efforts, and finally, the group that is measuring the efforts of the organization against the desired behavior and making whatever adjustments are necessary. Eventually, if the organization achieves the desired behavior, the need for the Center of Excellence may go away, as the behavior that they helped encourage has now become second nature for the organization.

Review Boards

Another approach to SOA governance focuses exclusively on the enforcement of the policies that have been outlined through the use of review boards. Many organizations already have formal review processes in place; therefore it makes some sense to extend the policies enforced by the existing review boards.

For example, it is very likely that your organization already has a review board that approves projects. This review board may currently focus on the financial side of the proposed projects in making their approval decisions. That review board can now factor in the business domain models to determine the architectural fit of the proposed project in addition to the financials of the proposal. This may require adding members to the approval process that are familiar with the architectural side of the equation, or it may require educating the existing members on the importance of the domain models.

The same thing holds true for architectural reviews and design reviews. The challenge for these reviews is the opposite of the project approval review. In that review, we needed to augment the process and optionally the people to take more technical issues into account. In the case of architectural and design reviews, the review board likely already covers many of technical issues, but is not properly positioned to handle organizational issues or scoping issues that may arise from applying the policies to the projects.

The biggest challenge with this approach to SOA governance, however, is that there are significant gaps. First, who is responsible for establishing policies in the first place? More often than not, review boards are responsible for enforcing policies but don't normally set them. At best, they may make decisions on the fly where policies don't exist, but even then, the reasons for the decision are unlikely to turn into official policy. In order to address this gap, some other authority in the organization must establish the policies that are enforced by the review boards. This will likely be an existing organization like Enterprise Architecture or a cross-functional group like a Center of Excellence.

Common Challenges

Regardless of the organizational approach chosen, there are several challenges that must be factored into your decisions around your organizational approach. The first is the risk of focusing too much on enforcement, and not enough on education on what the desired behavior is. When people don't understand the reasons why policies exist, they are likely to resist them when they see them as getting in the way of their responsibilities. When educated on the reason for the policies and the desired outcome that they are intended to achieve, they are more likely to be compliant with the policies. As stated earlier, the easiest way to achieve compliance is to make compliance the path of least resistance.

The second challenge is in picking governance processes that are inconsistent with the existing culture of the organization. If your organization is very consensus driven, an enforcement process that places extensive power in the hands of a few, such as with a review board, can be very risky. A strong focus on education, allowing key members to influence and persuade others in the process that establishes consensus may be easier for the organization to digest. If your organization is accustomed to a command-and-control structure, then yielding power to a few individuals and giving them authority to stop projects in their tracks may be possible. This is not to say, however, that matching the existing culture is always a good thing. Sometimes, the existing culture may be the biggest problem. Remember, SOA governance is about achieving a desired behavior in your SOA adoption efforts, and it is very likely that the desired behavior is different from what you are doing today. If the culture needs dramatic change, then dramatic changes in governance may be required. Frequently, however, this may require a change in leadership. It is typically very difficult for existing leadership to make dramatic changes in the behavior of an organization.

The next challenge is remaining relevant. A Center of Excellence is not the only approach that must be concerned about the engagement model with the rest of the organization. Enterprise Architecture is commonly at risk of becoming an ivory tower if they do not remain engaged with project activities. A review board is at even more risk, since they normally may not even meet with each other except when reviews are occurring. The team establishing policies must remain engaged with the teams that are expected to be compliant with those policies. An approach that strives to educate and mentor first, and then reviews and accepts/rejects second is more likely to be accepted, and more likely to have a higher compliance rate.

The final challenge is in matching the needs of all areas of the organization. While smaller companies may be able to have a single approach to SOA, larger companies with multiple lines of business may have different desired behaviors for each line of business. For example, if a company is focused on rapid growth in one line of business, but cost containment in another line of business, embracing policies that require company-wide standardization may help the second line of business cut their costs, but may severely restrict the ability of the first line of business to grow rapidly. Preferably, these goals are captured in the business domain models, however, they might not always be, or more likely, the domain models may not exist until further down the SOA journey. SOA must be business driven, and the behaviors, policies, and processes all must be reflective of those business goals.

Policies

The second piece of SOA governance is policies. Policies are the standards and guidelines that guide the staff associated with SOA towards the desired behavior. There are three key timeframes that have been addressed in the book:

1. During the processes associated with determining what IT projects to fund and execute: These processes are frequently associated with the broader subject of IT governance. While SOA governance should not introduce new governance processes associated with deciding what projects to fund and execute, policies associated with SOA governance should be included in the criteria. Surprisingly, vendors that offer tools in the SOA governance space do not have a term for this timeframe. We will refer to this as pre-project governance.

2. During project execution: In the vendor community, this is frequently referred to as design-time governance, however, the scope of SOA governance is certainly broader than just the design activities of a project. We will refer to this as project governance.

3. During the operation of production systems: In the vendor community and in this book, this timeframe is referred to as run-time governance. As long as there are services running in your production systems, there is a need to govern the interactions between consumers and providers.

Pre-Project Governance

During this timeframe, the desired behavior is centered on a simple concept: building the right thing. The decision-making process that results in an approved and funded project is what sets the initial scope for the effort. This initial scope has a significant impact in determining the artifacts that will be produced. If the scope incorporates an enterprise viewpoint appropriately, an organization may quickly build up a library of services whose expectations for reuse and agility in times of change have been well thought out. If the scope does not incorporate enterprise viewpoints and needs appropriately, it creates a risk that the artifacts developed will struggle to provide value outside of the initial project.

Artifacts

In order to perform pre-project governance, the following artifacts are recommended:

*   Organization Chart
*   Business Domain/Capability Models
*   Business Process Models

- Application Portfolio
- Service Portfolio

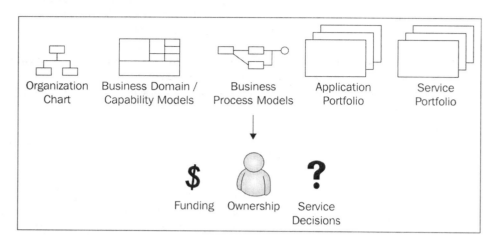

The first artifact, the **Organization Chart**, is a key element in how projects get defined. Normally, relationships with areas of the business outside of IT are highly influenced by the organization of the IT department. Change the organization of the IT department and you may change the way relationships are formed and managed with the rest of the business. The same also holds true with the organization of the rest of the business. Change the organizational structure of the business, and it's likely that the IT organizational structure will change with it.

The reason why the organizational chart is so critical is because there is normally a direct relationship between budget and organization. If a particular department in the business is in control of their own budget, it could be a big barrier to either creating services that will be used by other departments, or in using services that are managed by other departments. In the first scenario, many budget owners may want other organizations to contribute to the cost of development or maintenance of services if they use them. In the second scenario, they may be asked by those organizations to contribute to their costs. In addition, the projects that are proposed may have dependencies that other organizations must deliver in order to be successful. Depending on the state of relationships in the organization, this could be a major hurdle to overcome.

The thing to remember when adopting SOA is that it will likely put pressure on the existing organizational structure. If it doesn't, there are number of possibilities. First, your organization may already be aligned along the concept of service consumers and service providers. Second, your organization may not let organizational boundaries get in the way of doing the right thing. Finally, it may be that your SOA efforts are working too much within the boundaries of the organization and not really creating the type of change possible with SOA.

The next three artifacts, **Business Domain/Capability Models**, **Business Process Models**, and the **Application Portfolio** are closely related. These are analysis artifacts that should be used to guide the decisions on what services should be created. At a minimum, as discussed in the Advasco example, some form of domain/capability models and business processes models should be leveraged. Business process models on their own create a risk for creating process silos; just as many organizations today have application silos based upon their application portfolios. When business process models and application portfolios are combined with a domain/capability model, the resulting combination can be a powerful tool in guiding the decisions on what services should be established.

The final artifact, the **Service Portfolio**, is frequently a catalog of services that have been built and are available in production, but it is much more powerful when it is used as a planning tool. When the organization has taken the time to perform business process analysis and business domain/capability analysis, an outcome should be the definition of key services that the organization needs to create to fully leverage SOA.

Policies for Pre-Project Governance

The following are questions or policies that you should consider in your pre-project governance efforts:

- Has the proposed project identified candidate services?
- Has the proposed project mapped candidate services to the business domains as represented in the business domain/capability models?
- Has the proposed project reviewed the service portfolio against the list of candidate services?
- Has an appropriate team of project stakeholders been identified based upon candidate services?
- Has the proposed program/project been appropriately structured and scheduled to properly manage the development and integration of new and existing services?

- Have all funding details been determined based upon the services proposed and the organizations involved?
- Does the roadmap include the development of services with high potential for reuse?
- Are projects encouraged to reuse existing services, where appropriate, based upon the business domain models and business objectives?
- Are projects allowed to create redundancies, where appropriate, based upon the business domain models and business objectives?
- Have existing systems been taken into account in the definition of the proposed services?
- Is the organizational structure being reviewed on a regular basis based upon continued service analysis?
- Does the organization have a clear approach to resolving service ownership models?
- Are business processes properly leveraging services?
- Does your service portfolio properly account for any globalization impact?
- Does the service portfolio properly account for any planned areas for growth by acquisition?

Remember, this phase is the key timeframe to ensure that the organization builds the right services. If the decisions on what services to build are not investigated until after projects have been defined and funded, constraints will already exist that can be an impediment to building the right services.

Project Governance

During this timeframe, there are two major concerns: building the right services and building those services the right way. While the pre-project governance efforts are supposed to focus on building the right services, all too often, the proper artifacts are not available to make the necessary decisions at the time projects are approved. As a result, the necessary analysis and the decisions associated with the project architecture are performed within the project itself. This creates some risk, because the project does establish constraints that may get challenged by the results of analysis and architecture.

Like the architecture decisions that are made prior to project approval, the architecture and design activities must incorporate enterprise viewpoints and needs appropriately. For this purpose, the artifacts and policies mentioned as part of the pre-project governance all still apply. Besides these concerns, this timeframe is where an organization must ensure that services are built the right way.

Artifacts

In order to perform project governance, the following artifacts, besides those already mentioned in the pre-project governance section, are recommended:

- Service Technology Reference Architecture
- Service Security Reference Architecture
- Service Blueprints and Frameworks
- Standard Information Models and Schemas

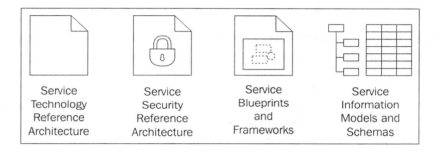

These artifacts are only the ones that have an impact on SOA governance. Clearly, there are many other artifacts that are associated with general development governance, but those that are not specific to service development and integration are outside of the scope of this book.

Service Technology Reference Architecture

The first artifact is the **Service Technology Reference Architecture**. The purpose of this artifact is to ensure that the appropriate technologies are used for the service being developed. The document should first define the appropriate service types for the organization and then map those types to specific service technologies. The document should never have more than one type mapping to the same set of specific service technologies. If multiple types map to the same set of service technologies, it may create more confusion than clarity. While those service types may be useful in determining service ownership, this document is focused on determining service technologies. On the flip side of things, enterprises with centralized infrastructure will also want to ensure that there is only one set of service technologies for each service type. For example, there will always be a catchall type, like "General Business Service" that will map to an application server and its associated service framework. Is it good to have both a .NET platform running on Windows Server and a Java EE application server running on a Linux platform? The correct answer is it depends. If your organization was a Microsoft development shop, but then acquired another company that was a Java development shop, it may make sense to have two general business service platforms. If both these groups still maintain their own data centers and operations staff after acquisition, there aren't too many issues. If, instead, the acquisition results in a consolidation of data centers and reduction in operational staff, justifying the continued operation of both platforms will be much more difficult.

Here are some service types that you should consider. Each one has the potential for being mapped to a specific set of service technologies.

- **Composite Services**: These are services that are built by combining the output of two or more services, and aggregating the respective responses into a single response.

- **Automated (Orchestrated) Processes**: These are services that are built by executing a fully automated sequence of actions as represented in a graphical process model. Technically speaking, a composite service is normally a specialized case of an orchestrated process, but if you choose to leverage very specific technologies for narrow service types, it is possible that you may need to define both service types and their associated service platform and technologies.

- **Integration Services**: These are services whose whole purpose is to service enable some system that does not support the standards required to speak natively to service consumers.

- **Presentation Services**: These are services that provide information in a presentation-friendly format. They don't actually produce the end user interface, but they provide the information in such a way that it is easily consumed by user interface technologies. This may require a slight variation of the standard service platform.

- **Management Services**: These are services that expose management and administrative functionality. In the past, there have been management-specific technologies including SMNP and JMX. Today, there are increasing numbers of products that expose management interfaces as SOAP or XML/HTTP interfaces, however, the use of SMNP and JMX are still far more prevalent.

- **Information Services**: These are services that are used to retrieve information from a variety of data sources, aggregating the results into a single response. Vendors typically market solutions in this space as data service platforms or data integration platforms. These services differ from composite services in that they are specifically designed to talk only to data sources on the back end, rather than any arbitrary web service.

- **Content Subscription Services**: These are services that provide content feeds, typically adhering to feed syndication standards such as RSS and ATOM.

- **General Business Services**: This is the catchall category for any service that doesn't fit into any of the other categories.

When mapping these service types to technologies, the following things must be considered:

- **Service Platform**: The technology decisions start with an underlying hosting platform. Typical choices include a Java Application Server, Windows Server, a Data Integration/Services Platform, a BPEL-based orchestration platform, and some ESB offerings.
- **Service Communication Technology**: The communication technologies are the protocol used to interact with the service. This includes both the message format used, such as POX, SOAP, or RSS, and the underlying message transport (HTTP, WebSphere MQ, or Tibco JMS).

For example, using the service types listed, a mapping to service platforms and communication technologies could look like this:

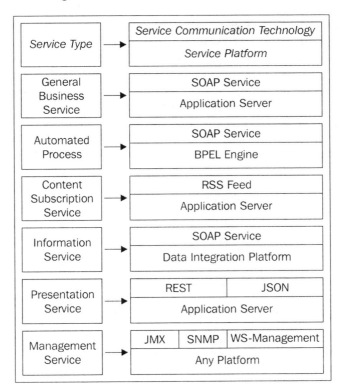

Beyond the mapping of service types to service technologies, the service reference architecture must also address policies associated with the message itself that go beyond the core communication technology. This can include naming conventions for URLs, namespace conventions for the XML messages, references to a canonical model, or more. It must also provide policies on how the non-functional capabilities associated with services interactions will be provided by the underlying infrastructure. This includes:

- Security (see Service Security Reference Architecture)
- Routing and load balancing
- Transport and mediation
- High availability and failover
- Monitoring and management
- Versioning and transformations

These non-functional capabilities are a key aspect of SOA, because they are the foundation of run-time governance. At the same time, they must be factored into the design-time decisions, because if the development teams don't utilize the technology appropriately, the ability to enforce run-time governance policies will disappear. If a team chooses to build its own security implementation or hard code rules for versioning into the implementation, it will likely require a code change and the associated release process to implement and enforce the policies in a service contract for a new consumer, increasing the time and effort required to bring new consumers online. We want to strive to implement these non-functional capabilities through policy-driven infrastructure that is configured, rather than coded.

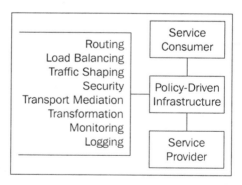

Service Security Reference Architecture

The next artifact is the **Service Security Reference Architecture**. This can be included as a subset of the Service Technology Reference Architecture, or created as a standalone artifact. Regardless of the approach, there are two questions that must be answered by the reference architecture:

1. What security policies must be enforced?
2. What technologies are used for enforcing those policies?

The first question must guide the developers of services and their consumers on security policies for authentication, authorization, encryption, digital signatures, and threat prevention.

There are two components to authentication. The first is a simple policy that states whether or not identity is required on all service invocations. It is strongly recommended that this is the case. With this policy in place, your organization must then specify what constitutes identity. It can be a user's name, an application's name, a company's name, or any combination of them. It may include additional attributes such as group membership or more. The one thing it should not be is anonymous. Companies must assume that in the future many services will comprise a particular interaction, with multiple teams involved. If identity on messages does not exist, it makes it extremely difficult to enforce run-time governance, since identity is what ties an interaction back to a service contract, as well as making the debugging process much more costly should problems occur in production.

With this identity specified, the next step is to decide when authentication is required on service invocations. Unlike a web application that faces an end user, one cannot assume that a simple challenge can be issued to allow a consumer to specify credentials on demand. When dealing with system-to-system interactions, it is very unlikely that the service consumer has access to the password of the user associated with the current thread. If passwords are not issued, then there needs to be a way to ensure that the credentials passed on the request have not been forged. For internal consumers, many organizations choose to only validate that credentials are from a trusted source, rather than performing an authentication on every request. This, of course, assumes that an authentication was performed at the user interface of the system.

Authorization, on the other hand, should always be performed on all service requests. Besides stating this policy, the reference architecture must also cover whether role-based or user-based authorization will be leveraged. Role-based authorization is generally preferred, as the management of policies associated with individual users can quickly become an impossible task for large organizations.

At first glance, you may first think that encryption is only concerned with the protection of sensitive data from systems that have no need for accessing it, but the certificate exchange associated with bi-directional SSL communications can also be leveraged to ensure that service endpoints only accept connections from authorized points on the network. For example, if you are leveraging an XML appliance as a policy enforcement point, it is possible for a rogue consumer to circumvent the appliance by entering the hostname or IP address of the service endpoint directly. By forcing a bi-directional certificate exchange between the XML appliance and the service endpoint in order to exchange service messages, these rogue consumers would be prevented from accessing the service, since they would not have the certificate required.

Digital signatures are a means of ensuring that the service messages have not been modified en route. While this is typically not used with internal consumers, it is frequently used when dealing with external consumers or external service providers, especially when those requests are sent over the open Internet. It may also be required on internal messages to ensure that some portion of the message, such as identity credentials, is coming from a trusted source.

Finally, threat protection is concerned with preventing consumers from exploiting a variety of techniques that can compromise the security of the service provider. Common examples include checking for SQL injection or detecting harmful XML messages, such as ones that are compliant with the XML schemas involved, but exploit recursion or buffer overflows to attempt to crash the server that will process the message.

The second question deals with the specific technologies associated with enforcing those policies. This begins with the service messages themselves. While the reference architecture has previously specified what constitutes identity, it must now say how that identity is represented on service messages. Will it be issued in plain text in a standard location? Will it be specified using transport-specific mechanisms (for example, HTTP headers) or as part of the actual message payload? The most flexible mechanism available today is only associated with SOAP messages, and that is the WS-Security framework. This framework establishes a standard location in the SOAP header for credentials, and provides a framework for specifying profiles that allow different token types to be used. Standard profiles include the Username profile (simple plaintext and hashed credentials), the **SAML (Security Assertion Markup Language)** Token Profile, the X.509 Token Profile, the Kerberos Token Profile, and the **REL (Rights Expression Language)** Token Profile. Not all products support all of the profiles, so be sure to dig deeper when a product claims to have WS-Security support. It may only support one or two of the token profiles, or potentially none at all, since WS-Security also specifies standard ways of handling message encryption and digital signatures.

Once the policies for the messages themselves have been set, the reference architecture must address the specific infrastructure associated with the enforcement of those policies. Will a standalone gateway, such as some ESBs or an XML appliance, be used to enforce authorization policies? If so, then all service traffic must be routed through those gateways, and techniques must be leveraged to prevent rogue consumers from circumventing those gateways. While a policy may say that SAML assertions must be used, how does a developer of a service consumer place those assertions on a message? Are they responsible for writing the code to do so, or will a framework be provided for them? If a framework is used, must the developer explicitly reference it, or will the insertion of credentials happen implicitly? The security reference architecture must provide enough information so that the developers of a service consumer or service provider know exactly what is required of them in their coding efforts versus what must be simply configured as part of establishing a service contract.

Service Blueprints and Frameworks

When trying to guide people to the desired behavior, a very powerful technique is to simply give them examples of it. This is the role of service blueprints. The reference architectures discussed can contain a large number of policies that can seem daunting to a developer, creating the risk that they get ignored. By creating blueprints that show a common pattern, and preferably the simplicity associated with following the pattern, developers are more likely to follow the guidelines.

For example, if your organization will be exposing external services, a challenge may be the propagation of identity to back-end systems, since identity checks may occur in a DMZ or through federation, yet the back-end services have no access to those identity stores. A blueprint can be created that demonstrates how that original identity flows through the connections required, and what code is required at each step (if any) to ensure it happens.

Blueprints also provide a convenient way of demonstrating how to choose within alternate strategies for a given service type. For example, a general business service may be accessible by either asynchronous messaging via message-oriented middleware, or via a synchronous messaging approach over HTTP. When should one be used over the other, and what are the differences in how to leverage them?

The second key piece of this artifact is service frameworks. While the underlying service platforms typically include frameworks for doing HTTP communication, XML message processing, and SOAP processing, it doesn't mean it's easy to use. This is especially true for security. While many frameworks can construct a SOAP message through the use of a wizard or code generator and one or two lines of code, adding a SAML assertion to that SOAP message can be much more complicated. A common theme with governance is that if you make compliance the path of least resistance, you're more likely to get compliance. If you have a policy that all service messages must contain identity, providing a framework so this can be done in one or two lines of code, or zero if possible, will ensure that your developers are compliant with the policy, versus requiring them to research SAML libraries and write many lines of code to make it happen.

Standard Information Models and Schemas

The final artifacts that are imperative for design-time governance are standard information models and schemas. A common goal associated with SOA is reuse, but reuse becomes much more difficult when common information is not represented consistently. For example, if there are two services that both need to deal with Account information, but both services represent that information in different ways, any consumer that needs to use both of those services must now implement logic that translates between the two definitions of Account.

In order to prevent this situation from becoming rampant, an organization must take this decision out of the hands of individual projects, and put it into the hands of a group with broader focus, whether that is the entire enterprise, or some larger domain. It is important that this group (or groups) understands that the goal is not to come up with the one universal representation that everyone agrees on, because odds are it doesn't exist. Rather, the goal is to minimize the number of representations for common information. If it can be one, that's the optimal point, but if it winds up being three or four, and we provide mechanisms for easily translating between them that is a big improvement over leaving it in the hands of every individual service consumer or service provider.

One factor that can play a key role in defining these models is the existence of industry standards for the information domains involved. For example, there are many messaging standards that exist for various verticals, such as financial services (SWIFT, ISO-20022), healthcare (HIPAA), and insurance (ACORD), which have been created for the explicit purpose of information exchange in business-to-business interactions. These schemas can be an excellent starting point for establishing internal standards, and should definitely be leveraged when exposing services externally. A second factor is the organization's use of third-party solutions, such as a major ERP product like SAP or Oracle. These systems often come with information schemas pre-packaged. The more customization to these schemas that you do, the more difficult it may be to upgrade that infrastructure. As a result, these schemas may also be a good starting point for establishing your own standards. The best scenario is where an industry standard exists that is independent of any third-party application, but supported by those third-party applications. That maintains independence from the vendor solution, yet leverages a schema with broad adoption in the industry.

Just as with the security reference architecture, the information models and schemas must make sure that they not only provide the standard models, but sufficient instructions on how to utilize them in service traffic. For example, if there was a common XML schema file for Account information called `account.xsd`, organizations should not allow individual projects to copy that file into their own projects. Rather, their projects should reference that schema file from some location that will be universally available. That allows the schema to be maintained and updated centrally, rather than having to go out to each individual project and update the Account definition one at a time.

Policies for Project Governance

The following are questions/policies that you should consider in your project governance efforts, in addition to all those that were specified in the pre-project governance if not enforced at that time:

- Have all services been mapped to an appropriate type?
- Are the service technologies chosen for each service consistent with the type to technology mapping specified in the reference architecture?
- Does the service use the standard communication technologies specified in the reference architecture?
- Does the service interface comply with all naming conventions for URLs as specified in the reference architecture?
- Does the service interface comply with all namespace conventions as specified in the reference architecture?
- Does the service interface properly reference all external schema definitions, rather than copying them locally?
- Does the service interface use the standard schema definitions properly?
- Do external facing services only expose industry standard schemas, where they exist?
- Is the service interface compliant with industry standards, such as WS-I?
- Does the service require identity on its messages?
- Are all service consumers properly specifying identity on outgoing requests?
- Have appropriate authorization policies been established for the service?
- Is the service communication infrastructure being leveraged appropriately?
- Are all internal consumers properly leveraging the standard service frameworks?

- Are all internal providers properly leveraging the standard service frameworks?
- Is all sensitive information properly encrypted according to the service security policies?
- Have service contracts been established between all consumers and providers?
- Are all aspects of the service contract fully specified including message schemas, versions, delivery schedule, points of contact, and expected usage rates?
- Have all services been thoroughly and adequately tested, with testing results available to service consumers, if required by the service contract? For internal consumers, testing results should always be available to help counter the natural tendency for developers to resist using things they didn't personally write.
- Have service managers been assigned for all new services?
- Are the service boundaries identified in the solution consistent with the business domain models?
- Has the solution incorporated existing services appropriately?
- Has the solution properly published information about new services into the Service Registry/Repository?
- Has the solution avoided creating redundant services that were not appropriate according to the business domain models?

Remember that all of these policies are in addition to policies that are already being enforced as part of your normal project governance process. Policies around coding conventions, project structures, code repositories, unit testing, integration testing, performance and capacity testing, and so on still apply.

Run-time Governance

During this timeframe, the major concern is the correct behavior of service consumers and service providers so that the infrastructure remains operational and in a healthy state at all times. There are two keys to this. The first is an accurate understanding of the role of infrastructure in the run-time environment at the time solutions are built, and second, is the appropriate use of the run-time infrastructure to enforce the policies established in the service contract. Unlike the other timeframes, there is really only one artifact that is used to describe the run-time behavior, and that is the service contract. Before covering that, let's first look at a conceptual view of the infrastructure and the guidance that must be given to teams during their design processes.

Policy-Driven Infrastructure

At its core, the run-time infrastructure consists of three things: infrastructure used to execute the logic associated with the service consumer, infrastructure used to execute the logic associated with the service provider, and infrastructure used to allow communication between the two. Earlier, it was stated that a goal should be to minimize the ways in which a service consumer and a service provider can communicate. Through the use of reference architectures, the policies are created that define these standards. With these standards in place, there are three core principles that should be adopted:

- Service consumers are responsible for ensuring that all messages they send are compliant with the service communication standards.

- Service providers are responsible for ensuring that they expose endpoints that can consume messages that are compliant with the service communication standards.

- The service communication infrastructure will enforce all non-functional capabilities for all messages that are compliant with the service communication standards, including mediation between those standards.

This results in a logical picture like this:

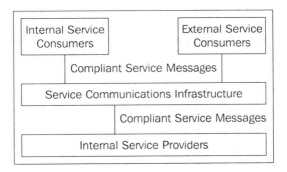

This clearly leads to a simple statement about run-time behavior: all service messages are compliant with the service communications standards. Unfortunately, that is seldom the case. If your organization leverages third-party products, it is unlikely that they will be compliant with all of your standards out-of-the-box. The key principle to follow, however, is that it is the responsibility of the non-compliant party to find a way to be in compliance, not the service communications infrastructure. Previous integration approaches, such as EAI technology, attempted to allow the endpoints to do whatever they wanted, and mediate between all of this in the middle. This quickly ran into problems, as precious CPU cycles were spent doing transformations and other activities to tie systems together which degraded the performance of other transactions that required little in mediation. The right approach is to push these adapters out to the endpoints, in an approach like this:

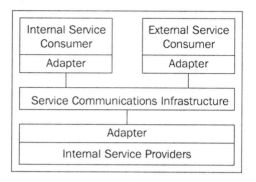

In this approach, it is the responsibility of the service consumer or service provider to put an adapter into their processing path prior to sending messages out through the service communications infrastructure. This can still involve EAI technology, but the use of that technology only accepts message traffic that is associated with the non-compliant system, versus dealing with all message traffic. These adapters can also be leveraged in process at the consumer or provider, such as using a third-party SOAP library within a Java execution environment that doesn't natively provide one.

The final adjustment to this diagram is to understand that the standards may be significantly different when dealing with an external party, whether that party is a service consumer or a service provider. This results in the following picture:

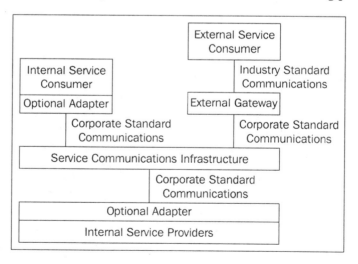

In this picture, an external service consumer communicates with an external gateway using industry standard communications technologies, both for the underlying transport as well as the messaging schemas. It is the responsibility of the external service consumer to be compliant with these industry standards.

The external gateway is responsible for the initial enforcement of security policies, as well as any mediation from the industry standards to the internal standards. Again, this encompasses both transport and messaging schema. If multiple versions of an industry standard exist, and are supported, the external gateway must be capable of transforming any of them into the approved internal corporate standards. If the internal standards are identical to the external standards, clearly this step is unnecessary. As a result, a best practice is to try to leverage industry standards for internal message formats as well, although it is recognized that this may require extending the standard for additional internal information.

Inside the corporate data center, all message traffic through the service communications infrastructure must be compliant with the corporate standards. Mediation within the corporate standards is a capability of the service communications infrastructure. This can include moving a message from an HTTP transport to a JMS-based transport (if both are allowed), mediating between POX/HTTP and SOAP/HTTP, and so on. It also includes mediation required for versioning of those standards. If the schema for an information entity has changed, but the use of a previous version is still allowed, the infrastructure should handle transformations between the two, when it is required.

It is the responsibility of the internal service consumer and the internal service provider to ensure that they are compliant with at least one of the standards for service communication. The endpoints do not need to support all of them, but they must support at least one. Where a service consumer or provider is non-compliant, they are responsible for employing an adapter, whether in process or an external entity for providing a compliant interface. Clearly, native compliance is preferable, as this prevents the proliferation of "glue" infrastructure used to tie everything together. The policies around service communication technologies should be used as part of your technology evaluation process for third-party packages to prevent this need as much as possible.

Service Contracts

With the standards for communication established, the infrastructure can now focus on the enforcement of the policies within service contracts. Some policies may be common to all service contracts, consistent with the policies that are in place in the reference architectures. For example, if the service technology reference architecture states that only XML payloads are allowed, this should be reflected in all service contracts. Any service message received by the communications infrastructure that does not contain an XML payload should be rejected.

While many of these policies can, and should be tested at development time, they must also be enforced at run-time, whether to deal with unknown bugs in the consumer or provider, protection against rogue applications that didn't follow appropriate testing procedures, or in case of external consumers, because we don't know what testing was performed at development time.

In addition, there are behaviors that cannot be handled by development time testing, typically associated with SLA enforcement point. A capacity test can be done to verify that the system behaves properly when 1,000 users of a service consumer are sending simultaneous requests, but this can't account for a mistake in analysis of the user base. If the real number is 10,000 users, how do we prevent the system from being overwhelmed? Each individual message may be fully compliant with all standards, but it's the fact that a much higher rate of message traffic is occurring that can create the problem.

The service contract must specify the expected usage by the consumer in an appropriate level of detail, as well as the expected response time from the provider when the system is behaving as expected. Additionally, thresholds for both usage by the consumer and response time from the provider must be established. Exceeding these thresholds results in notifications, allowing corrective action to be taken before a problem occurs, or a switch to a mode of self-preservation, where requests will be rejected in order to protect the back end service implementation from a complete failure.

The infrastructure must be capable of changing the policies associated with a contract, or establishing new contracts, without requiring a deployment of a new version of the service or the consumer solely for that reason. It is common that a change in contract may accompany an associated functionality change in a service consumer, service provider, or both, but it is the functionality change that drives the implementation change and the contract change. We never want a contract change to require an implementation change.

The service contract must also address reporting policies for service usage. The desired behavior at run-time should never be to deploy a service in production and then ignore it unless the system tells us otherwise. Usage reports should be provided to each consumer, as well as to the service provider. Analysis of these reports may trigger a change in policy, or even a need for a capacity modification, if the reports indicate the usage characteristics are changing.

Policies for Run-Time Governance

The following are questions or policies that you should consider in your run-time governance efforts:

- What is the normal rate of requests for a given service consumer?
- What is the expected response time for the service provider for typical requests from that service consumer?
- What actions are taken when the request rate for a given service consumer exceeds each of the agreed upon thresholds?
- What actions are taken when the response time for a given service consumer exceeds each of the agreed upon thresholds?
- Are there any time restrictions on when a particular consumer can access a service?
- For services with multiple entry points via different technologies (for example, SOAP/HTTP, XML/HTTP, SOAP/JMS), is policy enforcement defined and consistent (if needed) for each entry point?
- Are all security policies configured and being enforced?
- Are service requests routed to the appropriate version for each consumer, or have appropriate transformations been applied, preserving backward compatibility?
- Are all service messages being logged appropriately per any enterprise auditing requirements?
- Are all service messages being logged and preserved for the purpose of debugging?
- Are usage metrics being properly collected?
- Are usage reports being generated and distributed appropriately?
- Are the recipients of these reports properly reviewing them and accounting for any discrepancies in behavior?

- Are all policies associated with message structure being enforced by the run-time infrastructure?

- Are non-compliant messages being logged, rejected, and reported to appropriate personnel?

Remember that while the infrastructure can enforce many of the run-time governance policies, there is still a need to have people involved. If the staff deploys services into production and then forgets about them, there is significant risk of problems down the road. The lifecycle of a service consumer and a service provider must be managed from inception to decommissioning, not just from inception to production deployment.

SOA Governance Processes

Now that people and policies are in place, the focus turns to process. There are four major governance processes that need to be addressed:

- Establishing Desired Behavior and Policies

- Education and Communication

- Policy Enforcement

- Measurement

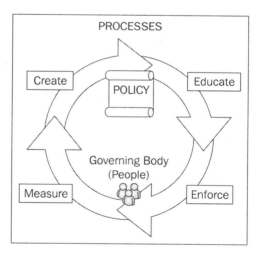

Establishing Desired Behavior and Policies

While most people immediately think of enforcement when they hear the word "governance" in the context of software development, this is not where governance begins. SOA governance begins by establishing the desired behaviors you want to achieve through your adoption of SOA. If there are no desired behaviors, how will you know if your SOA efforts are successful? Likewise, if the desired behaviors cannot be measured, how will you know if your SOA efforts are successful? "Increasing business agility" is not a behavior that can be easily measured. "Decreasing the average delivery time for IT solutions by 20%" is a behavior that can be measured. As you refine your desired behavior, keep in mind that SOA governance includes pre-project activities, project activities, and run-time activities, and your desired behavior should reflect all of these. The earlier behavior that discussed decreasing the average delivery time really only impact project activities. If there is a need to change the way IT solutions are defined, as was the case for Advasco, there needs to be a desired behavior that reflects this. Likewise, what is the driver for policy-driven infrastructure in support of service interactions? This could be a behavior related to the responsiveness of IT to business change, or it could be a behavior associated with the up time of the IT systems.

Once the desired behaviors have been established, then the organization can establish policies that will yield this behavior. In order to establish these policies, the roles described earlier must be considered, and responsibility given appropriately, whether that is through a cross-functional Center of Excellence or in a more decentralized manner where the individuals in those roles work together as needed to establish enterprise policies for pre-project activities, project activities, and run-time activities.

The importance of this step cannot be understated. All too often, the people acting as "governors" are put in place, but the policies (and sometimes even the desired behavior) are never established. This can result in a dictatorial style, where the "governed" can only guess what the governors are looking for, and those guesses are usually wrong. In addition, the outcome is completely dependent on the particular governor involved. Another potential outcome is where the SOA effort slowly fades into the background. Some teams may claim they are "doing SOA," but there's nothing to either support or refute the claim. Over time, people will simply stop paying attention, since the claim doesn't mean anything.

Education and Communication

Now that you have your desired behaviors and policies specified, the next process is still not enforcement, it is education and communication. While the governors may be aware of the policies, the governed may not be. In order to properly educate the staff, the people driving your SOA adoption efforts and establishing policy should also create a formal communication and education plan. The communication plan should include presentations that appeal to a broad audience, as well as presentations that are targeted toward particular audiences or toward a smaller group, such as an individual team. In addition to formal presentations, other communication techniques should be leveraged including whitepapers, blogs, and any other communication resources your organization has at its disposal.

Educational courses should be created for any skill sets the organization may lack, whether that is development technologies, such as Web Services, REST, or XML, analysis technologies, such as Business Process Modeling, or run-time management approaches such as ITIL v3 (**Information Technology Infrastructure Library**).

The people involved with your SOA governance effort must get the word out through presentations, documents, blogs, and whatever communication resources your organization has at its disposal. In addition to raising awareness of the effort, it will also build support for the effort such that people want to participate. People that may have questions about it will have the opportunity to voice those concerns, which can either lead to clarification on the reasons behind the policies, or to an adjustment of the policies. These conversations can be very constructive, because the policies must be connected to the desired behavior. If the connection between them is not clear, they should be questioned. If there is disagreement on whether the policy will lead to the desired behavior, alternative policies can be suggested, either by the governors or the governed. The one thing that is not questionable, however, is the desired behavior. For example, there should not be debate around the need to improve the average delivery time for IT solutions; however, there can be debate on the specific policies that will lead to that result.

Once again, there are strong parallels between SOA governance and traditional government. Constituents feel disconnected from their government when there is insufficient education and communication about the activities of the government. At its extreme, it can lead to a complete lack of faith in the government, which can have consequences ranging from revolt to the government becoming irrelevant. The same holds true for SOA governance. If the people involved in your SOA governance efforts are not educating and communicating, the people trying to make SOA a reality may simply ignore them or may be very resistant toward the enforcement efforts. Education and communication processes are the key to ensuring that governance is not seen with contempt in your organization, but rather as the key to enabling change for the better.

Policy Enforcement

The next process that must be addressed is the one that most people associate with governance, and that is policy enforcement. Regardless of how much you've educated your organization and communicated the desired behavior and policies, you still need to ensure that you have compliance with those policies, and that requires enforcement. First and foremost, you must remember the golden rule when it comes to any enforcement process:

 The easiest way to achieve compliance is to make compliance the path of least resistance.

Education and communication are a big part of this, but there are also many opportunities beyond this, especially for project governance and run-time governance. For example, if you have a policy that states that average response time must be collected for all services, the easiest way to ensure this happens is to make it a zero-effort activity for the service development team. Their service needs to be deployed onto an application server in a production environment to be used. If those application servers already have a service management agent deployed on them, that agent will recognize the new service and immediately begin collecting metrics and storing them in the appropriate repository, generating reports, and so on.

There will be policies for which some effort is required, but the burden should be on the people establishing the policies to ensure that the required effort is as minimal as possible. In the Advasco story, a policy was established that required service development teams to seek out potential consumers from outside the project at hand. If the team has to arrange for meetings with every development manager to discuss this, clearly, it's not going to happen. The managers will get tired of the meetings, and the development team will struggle trying to figure out who to talk to, while at the same time, they will be pressured by the project manager who is wondering what is taking so long. Instead, if the act of entering a proposed service into the Registry/ Repository kicks off notifications to other development managers, the effort can be significantly reduced. With appropriate analysis of the business domains and capabilities, the effort can be reduced even more by only sending notifications to managers most likely to be interested.

To further emphasize the need for the previous processes, enforcement processes can be streamlined when the people doing the enforcement are trusted to evaluate projects on their own. A possible approach recommended earlier was the use of review boards. Too often, review boards are only used because the policies have not been formally specified, and a room full of smart people is expected to make the decisions during the review process. This process is at risk for turning into a debate over policy between the people performing the review, rather than an effort to review and improve (if necessary) the project under review. By formally stating policies and educating the project teams with solid communication, the focus can get back to where it belongs—making the projects better or simply adding them to the list of compliant efforts and getting out of their way.

Measurement and Improvement

The final process associated with SOA governance is that of measurement and improvement. While policy enforcement can tell you whether your efforts are compliant with the policies or not, policy compliance alone will not tell you whether you're achieving your desired behavior. If you're not, then something needs to change. Your organization is adopting SOA because something needed to be improved. Governance guides the organization through that change. If, however, you don't get there, then something else needs to change, and it could be the governance itself.

At each step along your SOA journey, you should be measuring whether or not your SOA governance efforts are achieving the desired outcome. This includes:

- Ensuring that policies are established and documented.
- Ensuring that education and communication is relevant, understood, and successful.
- Ensuring that policy compliance is on an upward slope toward 100% at the rate desired.
- Ensuring that the measurable desired behaviors are being achieved. You could have 100% compliance, but still not reach the desired behavior.

If your measurements show a problem, then something needs to change. It can be a change in process, policy, or people. If the policy compliance rate is low, one should look at the effectiveness of the communication and education, as well as make adjustments to how policies are enforced. If policy compliance is high, but the desired behavior is not achieved, then perhaps additional policies are necessary. If the effort is in complete disarray, then perhaps new people are needed, or a new organizational approach, such as switching from an Enterprise Architecture-driven approach to a Center of Excellence. This cycle of continuous improvement can also be leveraged by the IT staff itself, to measure the effectiveness of the people providing SOA governance. If policies are causing undue pain for the staff, there needs to be a way to bring attention to it, and either lead to a change in policy or a change in people.

Simply put, if you are not measuring your efforts, there is no way to state whether your SOA adoption efforts are successful or not.

SOA Governance Technologies

There is no shortage of vendors in the marketplace that are marketing their technologies as SOA Governance solutions. It is important to know that you can't buy SOA Governance. What you can buy are solutions that make your governance processes more efficient, especially when it comes to policy enforcement. In Chapter 4, we introduced the concept of policy-driven infrastructure, which had the following key components:

- Policy enforcement points
- Policy decision points
- Policy information points
- Policy management points

Technology can help you in all of these domains, whether it is for pre-project governance, project governance, or run-time governance. The technology solutions that are available today include:

- Service Registry/Repository
- Service Testing Platforms
- Enterprise Service Bus
- XML Appliances
- Service Management Platforms
- Service Invocation and Exposure Frameworks

Service Registry/Repository

The Service Registry/Repository, in addition to tracking services and consumers, can assist you in the management and storage of policies associated with your SOA Governance efforts. It can easily play the role of a policy information point, and some products can also act as the policy management point. It is even possible to have it act as a policy decision point, although this is less common.

Being a repository, clearly the most value offered by a service Registry/Repository is as a policy information point. A core concept of SOA is that of the service contract, which is a collection of policies that govern a relationship between a consumer and a provider. These policies should be captured in the service Registry/Repository, as it needs to capture service consumers, service providers, and most importantly, the relationship between the two.

In addition to the policies that govern the interaction between a consumer and a provider, which are typically more concerned with run-time behavior, the Service Registry/Repository can also be a point where policies that apply at design time are captured. For example, a common policy associated with the design of SOAP-based interfaces is that the interface is compliant with the WS-I Basic Profile. This policy can be captured in the repository as something that must be enforced on all assets that have a type of SOAP Service.

For the pre-project governance phase, once again, the service Registry/Repository can be used to capture services from the moment they are first identified, regardless of whether any implementation of the service exists or any approved project exists to build an implementation. The service can simply be given a status of "planned" or "needed". From that point, new efforts that are seeking funding can take these services into account as they plan out their high-level architecture. Likewise, the repository can be a source of project ideas where a strategic service has been identified and entered into the repository, but no project has been proposed and approved to create it. These services would be entered into the repository as they are identified as part of the analysis efforts to define business domain models.

The service Registry/Repository can also be used to determine when the appropriate time is to decommission a service. By tracking the relationships and versions, and through integration with a service management platform that can assist in attaching actual dollar costs, candidates for decommissioning efforts can be more easily determined.

It is useful to think of the service Registry/Repository as a service lifecycle and portfolio management tool. From the perspective of the service provider, it is a tool for tracking each release of the service, the contracts with all of the consumers, as well as all of the corporate policies that apply to service design efforts. From the perspective of the service consumer, it's a way to easily find services that may be appropriate, keep up with the planned roadmap for services in use, and manage the contracts with each of those services. From the perspective of the enterprise, it provides a complete view of all of the consumers and services that are available, their roadmaps, as well as a view of services that haven't yet been created, but have been identified.

As a lifecycle management tool, the Registry/Repository can also be a trigger for events that cause policy enforcement as part of project time governance to happen. For example, when a service interface is defined and stored in the repository, this should trigger a review of the interface to check for compliance against the enterprise policies associated with service interface design.

The challenge for these tools is that there are very few standards for specifying policies and for interacting with a Service Registry/Repository. Standards such as UDDI and ebXML provide some guidance in interacting with the registry, but each tool is likely to have its own custom information model for how it represents policies. As a result, any policy enforcement point that wants to leverage a Registry/Repository as a policy information point will likely require custom integration work. All in all, the Registry/Repository is really the cornerstone of the infrastructure associated with SOA Governance. If a Registry/Repository does not exist, the individual enforcement points must each maintain their own record of the services involved. This cannot only lead to redundant data stores, but also to gaps in the data coverage where automated enforcement of policies may not currently exist.

Service Testing Platforms

The next piece of technology is a service testing platform. As the name suggests, these tools are focused on testing services. They may be sold as an add-on module or extension of a broader application testing platform, or they may be standalone solutions focused exclusively on services. In addition to being a tool that can automate the project-time compliance checks, they can also be a source of many "out-of-the-box" policies that can be reviewed by the people responsible for your SOA governance efforts and incorporated into the enterprise policies if deemed appropriate.

In addition to checking service interfaces for compliance with interface policies, service testing platforms also play a key role in the definition of service contracts. A service provider needs to provide baseline performance information for capacity planning purposes, the baseline's information can be captured consistently for all services through the use of a standard service testing platform. Furthermore, the testing platform can also be used to test service consumers and assist in the efforts to establish thresholds for notification and throttling. Once again, a standard tool for this purpose can be very advantageous. By preserving test scripts for each individual service consumer (which, incidentally, can be stored in a service Registry/Repository), capacity tests can be executed that include background traffic from other consumers, giving a more accurate picture of the behavior of the production systems.

As is the case with most of the tools discussed here, integration with a Service Registry/Repository is an important factor to consider. In order to automate enforcement of service interface policies, the Registry/Repository must be capable of kicking off compliance tests executed by the testing platform automatically kick of compliance checks against documented policies in at the time an interface definition is stored in the repository.

Enterprise Service Bus

The enterprise service bus, as discussed in Chapter 4, is primarily a policy enforcement point. All service traffic is intended to flow through the bus, making it an excellent place to enforce the policies associated with a service contract. An ESB can also be used to enforce some amount of project-time policies, simply because the ESB must be made aware of the service interface in order to make it available to service consumers. Normally, however, this takes place too late in the development process to be practical.

When evaluating enterprise service bus products, be sure to evaluate them from the perspective of policy enforcement points and service contracts. The product should provide a contextual model that easily allows the configuration of policies for the enforcement of service contracts. In utilizing an ESB, one must also be cautious to define your policies for run-time service interaction first, and then use the ESB to enforce them, rather than opening up the full range of capabilities of the ESB as the default policies for communication. Some ESB products have backgrounds in EAI technologies, and as a result, can still promote and integrate anything-to-anything mentality, which will not achieve any goals of reduced complexity in your environment.

XML Appliances and Security Gateways

XML appliances, also discussed in Chapter 4, are also policy enforcement points for run-time SOA governance. A difference between ESB products and XML appliances is that many ESB products tend to operate more like traditional software middleware. In fact, many ESB products have roots in EAI middleware technology. XML appliances, on the other hand, tend to have an operational model more similar to a network appliance than traditional middleware. Just as was recommended with ESBs, when evaluating these products, keep in mind the policy-driven mantra of configure, not code. Look closely at the contextual model of the appliance and how well it allows for the configuration of policies for the enforcement of service contracts between a service consumer and a service provider.

There is one additional differentiator between most of the XML appliances and the ESB products, and that is in the realm of security. At least two of the major XML appliances available took a path of supporting accelerated XSL transformation first, XML security second, and then full service intermediation third. As a result, the security features tend to be far more robust in the appliances, primarily in the area of threat protection. Threat protection is not normally something associated with a particular service consumer; rather, it is a set of policies that apply to all services, scanning all requests for malicious content, such as SQL injection. There are some consumer-specific policies that this enhanced scanning capabilities can enforce, however, such as a restriction on the size of the message. Two consumers using the same service could easily have very different characteristics in the message sizes. For example, in an ordering service, a key strategic partner may always have many line items per order, thereby increasing the size of a typical message from them, while a smaller partner may typically have one or two line items per order. Most appliances can handle policies on message size quite easily.

For both ESBs and XML appliances, a limitation is in the management capabilities. They typically have some elementary management capabilities, but if you require sophisticated management of the run-time behavior where complicated analytics are performed and then fed back into the enforcement points for SLA enforcement, you may need to look at the next type of product, a service management platform.

Service Management Platforms

Service management platforms, like both ESBs and XML appliances, are involved in run-time SOA governance, providing very similar coverage. These products may have fewer supported transport options than an ESB and fewer security capabilities than an XML appliance, but they typically provide more sophisticated management capabilities. Where ESBs and XML appliances can monitor and collect metrics, they typically only make these measurements available to some other analytics engine and/or dashboard. Service management platforms, however, include the analytics engine and dashboard. This analytic capability can allow the service management platform to inspect messages and track key metrics on a per service level, a per consumer level, per service broken down by consumer, and many other ways. It will also look at metrics from all monitoring points, so if you have a load balanced or clustered environment, you can see the rate of requests across all collection points, rather than seeing the rate of requests at one particular collection point. When enforcing the policies in a run-time service contract, this is an important consideration.

Furthermore, most service management products include both agents and gateways, which create additional flexibility in deployment. For example, most service management platforms include agents for ESBs; some even can work with certain XML appliances. Therefore, it is possible to use all three, leveraging ESBs where a large number of transports need to be supported and XML appliances at the perimeter for enhanced security, while deploying agents from a service management platform on both of them.

Service Invocation and Exposure Frameworks

Service invocation and exposure frameworks are a key part of the policy enforcement mechanism that may be overlooked. When Microsoft finally made a statement regarding products in the ESB space in 2005, they stated that the two key components of their solution were BizTalk and **Windows Communication Foundation (WCF)**. WCF is a framework for both invoking services and exposing logic as services. The biggest benefit of frameworks in the SOA governance space is that by using them, compliance with certain policies should be automatic. For example, if your organization has a policy on how identity should be represented on service messages, a framework can easily extract identity from the current consumer, format it in the appropriate way, and place it on the outgoing message. Depending on the framework involved, this may only involve a code annotation, a few lines of code, or perhaps nothing at all from the developer writing the service consumer. This certainly makes compliance the path of least resistance.

Summary

SOA Governance is a critical part of the SOA adoption effort. It begins with a concrete definition of what your organization hopes to achieve by adopting SOA, and then sets in place the people who will make the policy decisions that through effective processes, guide your organization to that desired outcome.

There is no one universal approach to SOA governance that works at all organizations, rather, the organization must take into account their own business structure, organizational model, and corporate culture in determining the appropriate way to drive SOA adoption, whether through Enterprise Architecture, a cross-functional Center of Excellence, or by simply relying on the organization as is to modify their individual behaviors to reach the goals desired.

The policy makers must address the desired behavior of the organization in defining and choosing what projects to execute, known as pre-project governance, the desired behavior of the project teams that are building the services and their consumers, known as project governance, and the desired behavior of those services, consumers, and the people that manage them at run-time as they execute in production.

However, stating policies are not enough. The organization must be educated on the desired behavior and the policies that will guide you there, and some amount of enforcement must be put in place to achieve compliance with those policies. Whether it is pre-project, project, or run-time governance, there are many technologies that can increase the efficiency of your compliance processes, whether through automated compliance checks, frameworks that guarantee compliance when used, or by simply raising the awareness through easy access to information about services and their consumers.

Ultimately, governance can only be effective if the organization puts measurements in place to judge whether or not the desired behavior is being achieved. Measuring compliance with policies is easy to capture, but if the wrong policies are put in place, the desired behavior will not be achieved. Governance is first and foremost about achieving the desired behavior. If policy compliance does not yield the desired behavior, then the policies may need to be changed.

As your organization proceeds along its SOA journey, the effectiveness of your governance processes can make or break your efforts. With good governance you can make your SOA efforts, and ultimately your business more successful, whether that represents some small changes in an organization that already works very well with its IT department, or a more fundamental change in the way the IT department works with the rest of the organization.

Cast of Characters

The following is a list of characters, in alphabetical order, that appear in the Advasco story, their role, and the chapters in which they appear.

Name	Role(s)	Chapters
Adil	IT Manager for Home Insurance Systems	2, 3
Alan	Project Manager, Brokerage Systems	5
Alex	Linux Operations Technician	6
Alexandra	Spencer's wife	2, 3
Andrea	CIO	3, 4, 5, 6, 7
Beth	Project Manager for Facilities Management	3, 7
Craig	Technical Lead, Customer Information Service	4
Ed	Analyst, Customer Information Service	6
Elena	Chief Architect	2, 3, 4, 5, 7
Greg	Member of Enterprise Architecture Team	3
Jared	Lead Analyst for Brokerage Services, Member of SOA Center of Excellence	3, 5, 6, 7
Jason	IT Manager for Auto Insurance Systems	4
Jennifer	Project Manager for Auto Insurance Systems	2
Jim	Project Manager for Pre-Qualification Service Manager for Portfolio Management Service	3, 5, 7
John	Member of IT Governance Board from outside of IT	5
Maria	Project Manager for Account Maintenance, Service Manager for Customer Information Service	3, 4, 5, 6, 7
Mark	Project Manager for Home Insurance Systems Service Manager for Customer Information Service	2, 5

Name	Role(s)	Chapters
Mike	IT Manager for Insurance Products	2
Mitch	Project Manager for Auto Insurance Systems	3
Paul	IT Manager for Home Insurance Systems	4
Raj	Technical Lead, Member of SOA Center of Excellence	3, 6, 7
Ramesh	Solution Architect for Annuity Systems	2, 4, 7
Ron	Member of SOA Center of Excellence	4
Ryan	Project Manager for Annuity Systems	2
Sarah	Middleware Operations Technician	6
Spencer	Member of Enterprise Architecture Team	2, 3, 4, 5, 6, 7
	Member of SOA Center of Excellence	
Tim	IT Manager for Auto Insurance Systems	2

Index

J

JBOS (Just a Bunch of Services) 29

K

key project roles, SOA journey 29

M

management 95
marketing 95
monitoring 94, 95

O

operational readiness checkpoint 66, 67

P

partner services, case study 123-133
people, SOA governance
  about 164
  business analyst 165
  enterprise architect/technology architect
    166, 167
  information architect 167
  IT manager 168
  organizing 171
  other stakeholders 171
  platform manager 169, 171
  security architect 168
  service manager/owner 169
  solution architect 165
  technical lead/domain architect 166
people organizing, SOA governance
  about 171
  center of excellence 173, 174
  challenges 175, 176
  competency center 173, 174
  enterprise architecture driven 172, 173
  review boards 175
PMOs 10
policies, SOA governance
  about 177
  pre-project governance 177-180
  pre-project governance, artifacts 177-179
  project governance 180, 189, 190

  project governance, artifacts 181
  run-time governance 190, 195, 196
policy-driven infrastructure, service
  versioning policies
  components 85
  conceptual view 92
  Enterprise Service Bus (ESB) 89, 90
  exposure framework 91, 92
  policy, applying 88, 89
  policy enforcement point 86
  policy information point 86
  policy infrastructure point 86
  policy management point 85
  service invocation 91, 92
  service management platforms 90, 91
  XML appliances 90
Portfolio Management Organizations.
  See PMOs
pre-project governance, artifacts 177
  application portfolio 179
  business domain/capability models 179
  business process models 179
  organization chart 178
  service portfolio 179
project governance, artifacts
  service blueprints 187
  service frameworks 187
  service security reference architecture
    185-187
  service technology reference architecture
    181
  service technology reference architecture,
    policies 184
  service types 182
  service types, mapping to technologies 183
  standard information models 188, 189
project inception checkpoint 119, 120

R

Representational State Transfer.
  See REST
REST 43
roles, enterprise SOA governance
  about 57, 58
  analysts 59
  business management 59

Thank you for buying
SOA Governance

About Packt Publishing

Packt, pronounced 'packed', published its first book "*Mastering phpMyAdmin for Effective MySQL Management*" in April 2004 and subsequently continued to specialize in publishing highly focused books on specific technologies and solutions.

Our books and publications share the experiences of your fellow IT professionals in adapting and customizing today's systems, applications, and frameworks. Our solution based books give you the knowledge and power to customize the software and technologies you're using to get the job done. Packt books are more specific and less general than the IT books you have seen in the past. Our unique business model allows us to bring you more focused information, giving you more of what you need to know, and less of what you don't.

Packt is a modern, yet unique publishing company, which focuses on producing quality, cutting-edge books for communities of developers, administrators, and newbies alike. For more information, please visit our website: www.packtpub.com.

Writing for Packt

We welcome all inquiries from people who are interested in authoring. Book proposals should be sent to author@packtpub.com. If your book idea is still at an early stage and you would like to discuss it first before writing a formal book proposal, contact us; one of our commissioning editors will get in touch with you.

We're not just looking for published authors; if you have strong technical skills but no writing experience, our experienced editors can help you develop a writing career, or simply get some additional reward for your expertise.

SOA Approach to Integration

ISBN: 978-1-904811-17-6   Paperback: 300 pages

XML, Web services, ESB, and BPEL in real-world
SOA projects

1. Service-Oriented Architectures and SOA
   approach to integration

2. SOA architectural design and
   domain-specific models

3. Common Integration Patterns and how they
   can be best solved using Web services, BPEL
   and Enterprise Service Bus (ESB)

4. Concepts behind SOA standards, security,
   transactions, and how to efficiently work
   with XML

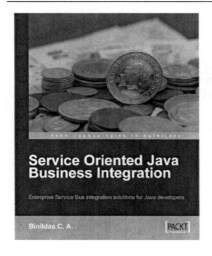

Service Oriented Java Business Integration

ISBN: 978-1-847194-40-4   Paperback: 414 pages

Enterprise Service Bus integration solutions for Java
developers

1. Vendor-independent integration of components
   and services through JBI explained with real-
   world examples

2. Hands-on guidance to ESB-based Integration of
   loosely coupled, pluggable services

3. Enterprise Integration Patterns (EIP) in action,
   in code

4. ESB integration solutions using Apache open-
   source tools

Please check **www.PacktPub.com** for information on our titles

Business Process Driven SOA using BPMN and BPEL

ISBN: 978-1-847191-46-5   Paperback: 328 pages

From Business Process Modeling to Orchestration and Service Oriented Architecture

1. Understand business process management and how it relates to SOA

2. Understand advanced business process modeling and management with BPMN and BPEL

3. Work with tools that support BPMN and BPEL (Oracle BPA Suite)

4. Transform BPMN to BPEL and execute business processes on the SOA platform

5. A complete business process management life-cycle

SOA and WS-BPEL

ISBN: 978-1-847192-70-7   Paperback: 250 pages

Composing Service-Oriented Architecture Solutions with PHP and Open-Source ActiveBPEL

1. Build Web Services with PHP

2. Combine PHP Web Services into orchestrations with WS-BPEL

3. Use better WS-BPEL to enable parallel processing and asynchronous communication

4. Simplify WS-BPEL development with free graphical tool ActiveBPEL Designer

Please check **www.PacktPub.com** for information on our titles

Breinigsville, PA USA
27 December 2010
252140BV00003BA/2/P

9 781847 195869